BERKELEY COUNTY

PALMETTO
PUBLISHING
Charleston, SC
www.PalmettoPublishing.com

Hardcover ISBN: 9798822960039
Paperback ISBN: 9798822968950

BERKELEY COUNTY

THE WINDS OF POLITICAL CHANGE

POST WW1 TO THE
21ST CENTURY

B. Earl Copeland

FOREWORD

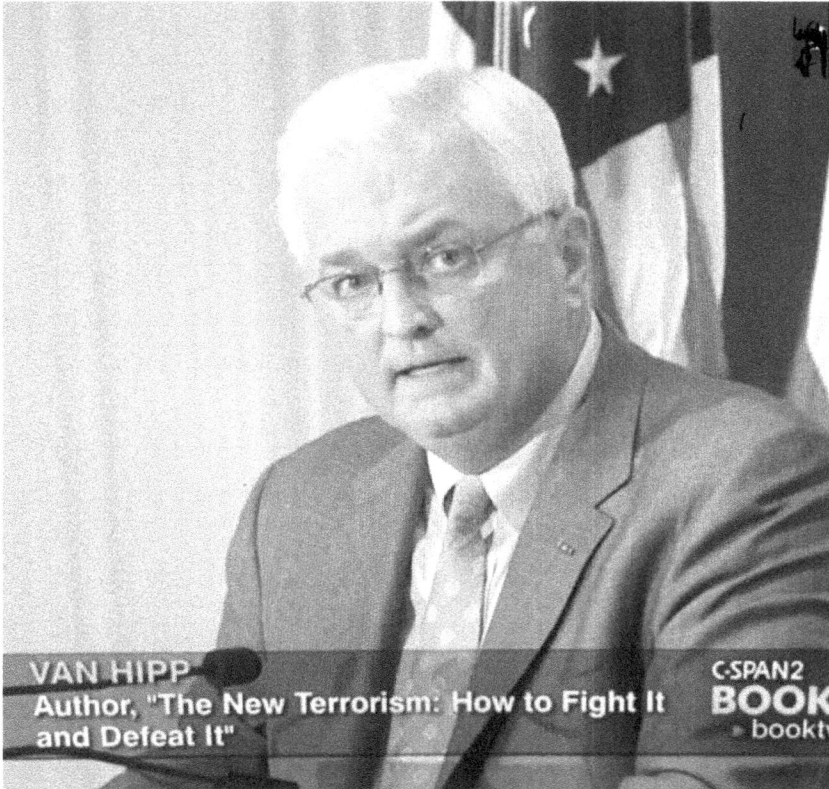

=-By Van D. Hipp, Jr.,

Former South Carolina Republican Party Chairman, former Deputy Assistant Secretary of the Army for Reserve Affairs, former FOX News Contributor on Defense Issues and CEO of American Defense International

Earl Copeland is the right person to tell the story of *BERKELEY COUNTY: Winds of Political Change*. As the Mayor of Hanahan, South Carolina and Chairman of the Berkeley County Republican Party, he had a front row seat. He also, through his drive, personality, leadership, and ability to bring people together, helped lay the foundation and inspire the "winds of political change."

Any student of South Carolina history will love the stories of the "Dennis Dynasty," Governor Carroll Campbell, and House Armed Services Chairman Mendel Rivers. Students of Berkeley County history will enjoy hearing about the roles that Henry Brown, Ray Isgett, Jim Rozier, Janet Brown Jurosko, and so many others played in building the current political landscape of Berkeley County.

And even the best student of South Carolina history, and particularly Low Country history, are sure to learn something new in Earl's book. For example, how many people today know that Mount Pleasant, SC was actually once the "county seat" of Berkeley County?

If a book talks about bootlegging whiskey and the Hell Hole Swamp, you know it's going to be a good one! This book does that, but it also accomplishes much in educating the reader on the politics of the Low Country and how Berkeley County came to be the vibrant, economic South Carolina powerhouse of approximately a quarter of a million residents that it is today.

Earl Copeland has done a wonderful job in writing *BERKELEY COUNTY: Winds of Political Change*. If you love the Low Country, politics, and history, you need to read it! I recommend it highly.

Van D. Hipp Jr.

ACKNOWLEDGMENTS

This book is dedicated to the many men and women of the Berkeley County Republican Party who have volunteered, and continue to volunteer, their time, energy and resources, and the voters who supported their labors, to give the citizens of Berkeley County the responsible government that we have today. And a special thanks to those who answered the call to serve our citizens in elective and appointive positions.

We are forever grateful to the wonderful people who contributed news clippings, photos, suggestions, and their support, all of which will give readers a more meaningful and interesting read and a better understanding of the monumental task of bringing about meaningful change. Some of those special people and entities who we wish to recognize are: Berkeley County Sheriff Duane Lewis, whose father, Solon "Sonny" Lewis, was a former Berkeley County deputy sheriff, the first Hanahan Police Chief and later Goose Creek Police Chief, and Sheriff Lewis' co-author of their book, *Lawmen and Lawlessness*; South Carolina Low Country Historian Dr. Michael Heitzler; Van D. Hipp, Jr.; Kathy Rozier; Dan Isgett; Suzannah Smith Miles; Mayor Gregg Brown and the Town of Ninety Six, South Carolina: Charleston County Public Library; Charleston Post and Courier; Charleston Magazine; Berkeley Independent News; Hanahan News; Goose Creek Gazette; And last, but not least, we want to recognize Nadine Copeland, wife of the author, who acted as proofreader and cheerleader while he pursued his passion of writing.

TABLE OF CONTENTS

ORIGIN AND HISTORY OF BERKELEY COUNTY, SOUTH CAROLINA

[1]Berkeley County was established in 1682. It was named after John and William Berkeley, co-owners of the Province of Carolina.[4] It became part of the Charleston District in 1769. It did not exist as a District during most of the 19th century and generally was part of the Low Country culture. In 1882, after Democrats regained control of the state legislature following the Reconstruction era, they established the current incarnation of Berkeley County, with its seat at Mount Pleasant. The county seat was moved in 1895 to Moncks Corner.[3]

---

1 WIKIPEDIA

★ ★

CHAPTER 1

Berkeley County - Wild and Lawless

★ ★

Dating from its earliest days after being established by the South Carolina legislature in the 1800s with county lines approximating its present-day boundaries, Berkeley County had a reputation of being wild and lawless. [2]In his new book, Lawmen and Lawlessness, Sheriff Duane Lewis captured the essence of the early days of law enforcement in Berkeley County.

He tells of the difficulty of the early Berkeley County sheriffs enforcing liquor laws in a county where many of the constituents of the county who elected the sheriff, were friends and families of some of the

---

2 Book – LAWMEN AND LAWLESSNESS by S. Duane Lewis and Constable Daniel J. Crooks

prominent citizens who also depended on the illegal liquor trade for income. At times it made for some interesting situations.

Photo; Courtesy Duane Lewis

The author of that book notes "The farmers' sparce income was honestly earned for the most part, but often it was necessary to dabble in the moonshine business, especially when kerosene or wool blankets were in short supply. Toting a load of liquor from Hell Hole to places like Moncks Corner, Goose Creek, or Ten Mile once a month helped make up for the shortages in income."

The Old Goose Creek Bridge across GC reservoir (NAD Road)
Photo: Courtesy Duane Lewis

He continues, "For others, illegal liquor was a primary source of income. With that money, the powerful moonshiners bought political power from Moncks Corner to the governor's office. Pervasive corruption began to slowly seep into local politics. By the 1920s, ordinary folks conceded that Berkeley County was just one big swamp, and Hell Hole was the county seat. Moonshine was the king that held reign over the county. For years Berkeley was known for little else. Men would be murdered, and careers ruined by the greedy passion for money." Berkeley County became known as "Bloody Berkeley".

Hell Hole Swamp in northern Berkeley was the moonshine capital of the south. Competing bootleggers operated their stills from Hell Hole, shipped their illegal liquor by automobiles modified to hide glass jars in any cranny they could find, behind seats, behind fake walls and special compartments under the vehicle.

Photo: Courtesy Duane Lewis

During the prohibition years of the 1920s and 1930s, they even shipped it by rail and trucks to the infamous gangster, Al Capone, in Chicago.

Infamous Gangster, Al Capone

[3]Stories abound about how racketeer Al Capone would arrive in a fancy limo with his henchmen and wads of money "to take care of business." Moonshine kingpins Glennie McKnight and Jerry "Foxy" Christian would buy all the corn whiskey they could from local bootleggers and ship it to Chicago in railroad boxcars. One yarn tells of the time Capone didn't pay for a shipment sent up by McKnight. When McKnight refused to send more, Capone supposedly sent six Cadillacs filled with his toughest hoods down to teach the Hell Hole moonshiners a lesson. McKnight's boys led the gangsters in their leather shoes and fancy suits into the swamp and left them there after taking their money and their cars.

---

3 Appendix O - Moonshine over Hell Hole - Charleston Magazine by Suzannah Smith Miles

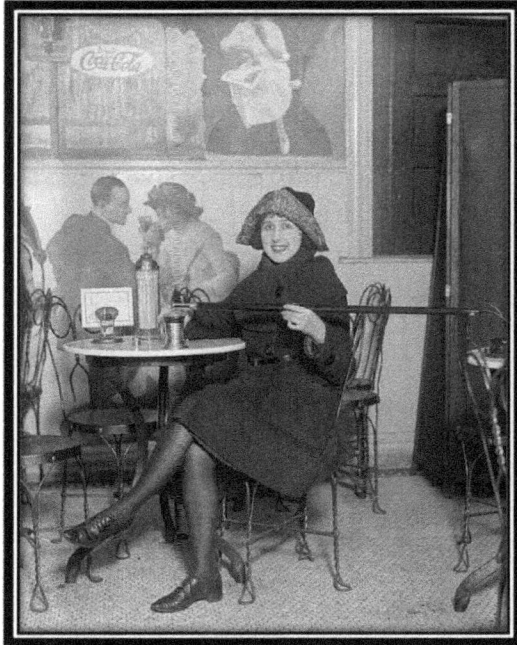

Photo: Courtesy Duane Lewis

[4]In May 1926, competition in the Hell Hole Swamp illegal liquor business reached a fever pitch. A large law enforcement raiding party gathered near St. Stephen in upper Berkeley County. Federal agent Seabrook, accompanied by five state constables, had learned from their informers that there was a large complex of stills "within shouting distance of each other" in Hell Hole Swamp.

Competing shiners in two automobiles were making their way from the Cordsville community, which is north of Moncks Corner, toward

---

4 Book – Chapter 36, LAWMEN AND LAWLESSNESS by S. Duane Lewis and Constable Daniel J. Crooks

Moncks Corner at a high rate of speed, with bullets flying back and forth. In the first car were Sam McKnight, Jervey Mitchum and Glennie Johnson, who were suspected of ratting to the lawmen who had just the day before destroyed the stills. In the second car were Jeremiah Wright, James Anderson and brothers Thad and Ben Villeponteaux.

Luck ran out for the occupants of the first car when they suddenly encountered a slow train across the tracks on Main Street in Moncks Corner. A shootout followed. When the dust settled, Sam Mcknight and Jervey Mitchell in the first car, and Ben Villeponteaux in the second car, all lay dead.

Competition between bootleggers was fierce in upper Berkeley, and the need for expanded markets led to regular sightings of shiners loaded with moonshine in Goose Creek and beyond.

CHAPTER 2

The Dennis Dynasty

Except for brief periods in the very early 1900s, and the period between the assassination of Senator E. J. Dennis and the election of his son, Rembert, for over sixty years Berkeley County was controlled by the [5]Dennis dynasty.

Edward James Dennis, Sr. was the first in the dynasty of Berkeley County senators, having served from 1894 until his death in office in 1904.

[6]Edward James Dennis, Jr., was second in the line. He was a member of the South Carolina state senate from Berkeley County, 1904-06, 1910-14, 1918-22, 1926-30.

---

5 Appendix A – 3 Generations of Berkeley Countiy Senators Dennis
6 PoliticalGraveyard.com

State Senator Edward James Dennis, Jr

Rembert Coney Dennis was the third, and last, in the dynasty. He was also, by far, the longest serving, having been first elected to the South Carolina Senate in 1942.

Rembert C. Dennis was born in 1915 in Pinopolis, S. C. to Edward James and Ella Mae Coney Dennis. He graduated from Berkeley High School, and while in school, worked for three years as a Senate page. He graduated from Furman University in 1936 with a B.A. degree. While at Furman, Dennis was elected President of the Student Council, played football, and ran track.

After graduation, he took a job with the U.S. Maritime Commission in Washington and began law school at Georgetown. In 1940, he received his law degree from the University of South Carolina. Upon his election to the South Carolina House of Representatives in 1938, Dennis became the third generation of the Dennis family to represent Berkeley County in the General Assembly.

In 1942, Dennis sought and won election to the South Carolina Senate, following his father and grandfather before him. Conscious that his action opened him to criticism as a slacker, Dennis recalled for oral historian Dale Rosengarten "I had a burning desire to fill the seat that my father had lost by assassination and my mother had lost because it was too early for women to be accepted for higher office.... It was my feeling that I was going to be severely criticized for running for political office when I was of the age that I was expected to be in military service.... I decided I would run and abide by the results and publicly stated that it was their [the public's] decision, and I would be a volunteer for service if I didn't win...."

[7]Senator Rembert Dennis was one of the most influential legislators of his time. His career spanned almost fifty years, in the South Carolina

---

7 Rembert Coney Dennis Papers, University of South Carolina

House of Representatives 1939-1942, and the South Carolina Senate, 1943-1988, when ill health forced his retirement from public life.

He suffered a heart attack in 1976 and was involved in two serious automobile accidents, in 1984 and 1985. He died in 1992. Thus ended the long rule of the Dennis dynasty.

The South Carolina state senate was changed from one senator per county as originally set up in the South Carolina Constitution, to single member districts that straddle county lines based on population. This change was brought about because of a U. S Supreme Court ruling that forced all states to redo state legislative districts to reflect its one man, one vote ruling.

"He walked with and was one of the giants in the South Carolina Senate, and when he left the Senate, it was truly the end of that era." Thus, Isadore Lourie characterized the passing of Rembert Coney Dennis (1915-1992). "Dennis was an able legislator, a coalition builder who promoted fiscal conservatism yet social progressivism. Between 1943 and his retirement in 1988, he ascended to lead the Senate, succeeding Edgar Brown as Chair of the Finance Committee in 1972, and in 1984, following the death of his close friend Marion Gressette, as President Pro Temp of the Senate. In recalling his ambition, Dennis commented that during the early 1950s — "I wanted to be governor, and then United States Senator. I thought I was a good candidate then for anything, but maybe President. But as I served, I learned. The more I learned, the more I found out the less I knew.... I thought, when I got to be Chairman of the Finance Committee, with my years of seniority, I was getting along about as good as the governor, but I had a desire to get into the national picture. I gave it up quickly when I got so busy as Senator, and Chairman of the Finance Committee."

Following Senator Rembert Dennis' retirement at the end of the 1988 session, State Representative Robert Helmly, a Berkeley County businessman, was elected Senator. He served as senator 1989-1993, when he chose to retire and turn his attentions back to expansion of his company, Home Telephone Company.

★ ★

CHAPTER 3

The Way It Was

★ ★

[8]"Do you mean to say you hired the king of the bootleggers to be a Prohibition officer?" gasped U. S. Senator K. D. McKellar of Tennessee, a member of the U.S. Senate's Brookhart Committee, which was investigating the numerous discrepancies uncovered with the Hell Hole Swamp raids. The more the Senate probed into the Prohibition-ignoring moonshiners of Hell Hole, the more they became displeased.

"Bootlegging continues," attested state constable J. L. Poppenheim. "McKnight may have cleaned up part of the county, but it didn't help much." Indeed, after McKnight turned in his badge, he went right back into the bootlegging business.

---

8 Appendix H - Moonshine over Hell Hole - Charleston Magazine by Suzannah Smith Miles

The findings of the Brookhart Committee's investigations and later hearings in Columbia brought even greater gasps of astonishment and not a few sniggers of amusement. It was becoming evident that law-enforcement officers, from sheriffs to deputies, had either been buying corn whiskey, selling it, or giving seized whiskey away to their friends. Even squeaky-clean Governor Richards became involved: His own son-in-law had been found transporting whiskey across the state after leaving a deer hunt near Hell Hole Swamp; four bottles of Hell Hole liquor had been put in his car trunk by Berkeley County deputy sheriff W. E. Woodward.

Enraged, Governor Richards ordered Sheriff C. P. Ballentine to fire Woodward. When Ballentine refused, Richards ordered Ballentine removed from office. Ballentine, who was an elected official, appealed to the Supreme Court, saying the governor did not hold such executive privilege. Meanwhile, the governor also accused Ballentine and Woodward of not only selling seized liquor but imbibing it themselves. In the end, the Supreme Court decided with the governor. Ballentine was out.

Clouds were also beginning to gather around Berkeley County's state senator, Edward J. Dennis, Jr. While the feds were still on the hunt, they called in Ballentine and Woodward to testify about what was really going on in Berkeley County. The real people in the whiskey business, they said, were none other than Senator Dennis and the state constables (purportedly members of the Anderson-Villeponteaux gang) who Dennis had personally asked the governor to appoint as Prohibition agents.

Ballentine's and Woodward's testimonies were damning. They explained how Dennis and his cronies were getting rich through a foolproof system that operated on many levels. It worked like this: The constables would arrest a moonshiner and seize his whiskey. They then sold the whiskey to their own bootleggers. Senator Dennis, who was a lawyer, made his money through attorney's fees when he represented the moonshiners who'd been caught. Given his influence, Dennis could arrange to have the cases dropped, but only for a "consideration." These fees, said Ballentine and Woodward, amounted to nothing short of paying tribute to the "king of the bootleggers."

A special investigator and prosecuting attorney were appointed. Indictments were issued against Senator Dennis and the constables. The trial was held in Charleston, with a long line of moonshiners parading across the witness stand, most of whom substantiated the charges.

It was all nonsense, testified the senator. "Who could believe bootleggers, anyway?" With a brilliant defense that included testimonies from congressmen and some of the foremost lawyers of the state, the jury eventually brought in a verdict of acquittal. Throughout it all, corn whiskey poured from the stills in Hell Hole Swamp. Raids continued but with the same ineffectual results. And the bitterness between rivals festered.

This came to bloody climax when, on the morning of July 24, 1930, as Senator Dennis was walking to his office in Moncks Corner, 30-year-old W. L. "Sporty" Thornley placed a shotgun on the radiator of his car and fired a load of buckshot into the senator's brain. The senator died the following day. Thornley was arrested, as was his brother, Curtis, and Fred Artis, the bodyguard of Glennie McKnight.

[9]Following WW1, Webster Lee "Sporty" Thornley suffered from "shell shock", which today is known as Post Traumatic Stress Disorder (PTSD), because of his service in the Army in the trenches of France. Most people who knew him thought he was crazy because at times he would have flashbacks of the war if something or someone startled him. He would hit the floor and crawl around. His service in the 42nd Army Division, known as the "Rainbow Division", left him mentally impaired and vulnerable to suggestions by those who did not wish him well.

Sporty, who was described in newspaper articles as a "tubercular and disabled, World War I veteran" and town loafer with the "intelligence of a boy of 12," later testified that it was Glennie McKnight who had furnished him with the gun. For shooting Dennis, McKnight had promised Sporty cash, protection, and a house for his family. McKnight was also arrested. Yet in the end only Sporty was convicted and given a life sentence." He was sent to the State Penitentiary in Columbia. Many years later he was released.

It was believed at the time, but not proven in court, that Sporty Thornley was telling the truth about being hired by Glenny McKnight to kill Senator Dennis. And rumors ran amuck, and were even published, that Senator E. J. Dennis was receiving money from some of the moonshiners,

After Senator Dennis' death, his wife was urged to run for his seat. She qualified to run, but she was defeated in the Democrat primary of 1930 by Marvin M. Murray. In those years winning the Democrat

---

9 Appendix H - Moonshine over Hell Hole - Charleston Magazine by Suzannah Smith Miles

primary was tantamount to being elected, since there was no serious competing political party to oppose the Democrat nominee in the November general election. Senator Murray served until Senator Rembert C. Dennis was elected to that seat in 1942.

CHAPTER 4

L. Mendel Rivers, U. S. Congressman

Another force in Berkeley County politics during the era of Post WW2, was [10]Lucius Mendel Rivers, a country lawyer and native of the St. Stephens area of upper Berkeley County. For over three decades, Mr. Rivers served the people of Berkeley County, the State of South Carolina, and the First Congressional District of South Carolina.

[11]Congressman Lucius Mendel Rivers was born on September 28, 1905, in the rural Berkeley County community of Gumville. He was the fifth child and second son of Lucius Hampton Rivers, a turpentine still operator, and Henrietta McCay. The family moved to North Charleston in 1916 following the death of Lucius Rivers and the subsequent loss of the family farm. Rivers attended the College of Charleston from 1926 to 1929. After his third year, he was admitted to the University of South Carolina School of Law. At the end of his second year he was last in his class and not invited back. Despite his lack of a degree, he passed the bar exam in 1932 by reading the law.

Rivers first ran for the state House of Representatives in 1932 but lost in the Democratic primary runoff. In 1933 he was elected in a special election to the state House. In 1934 he became chair of the Charleston County House Delegation receiving more votes than any other candidate. In 1936 he left the political arena and went to work for the United States Department of Justice in its taxes and penalties division. Rivers married Margaret Middleton in 1938. They had one son and two daughters.

Rivers returned to politics following the death of First District congressman Tom McMillan in 1939. In August 1940 he won the

---

10 Photo Credit: photograph by Warren K Leffler
11 Huntley, Will F. "Mighty Rivers of Charleston." Ph.D. diss., University of South Carolina, 1993.

Democratic primary, successfully defeating the Charleston "Ring" headed by Burnet Maybank. He was subsequently reelected to Congress fifteen times with only minor opposition.

As a freshman congressman, Rivers was appointed to the Public Buildings and Grounds Committee and the Merchant Marines and Fisheries Committee. In March 1941, however, he was appointed to the Naval Affairs Committee headed by Carl Vinson of Georgia. There, Mendel Rivers developed a career as a staunch supporter of the military and national defense. Following Vinson's retirement in 1965, Rivers became chair of the House Armed Services Committee, a position he held until his death.

Rivers was a conservative Democrat who was often at odds with his party. He frequently criticized American foreign policy, foreign aid, and the United Nations. He was a strong supporter of increased military spending and the establishment of a nuclear navy. During his years in Congress, the First Congressional District was a major benefactor of military spending. Major installations in the district included the Charleston Naval Base and Shipyard, the Charleston Air Force Base, the Navy Minecraft Base, the Ordnance Depot, the Marine Corps facilities at Beaufort and Parris Island, and a Veterans Administration Hospital. Vinson once jokingly told Rivers that if he put another thing down in his district it was going to sink.

While Rivers was seen as an advocate of the little man, he was also a segregationist. He supported the States' Rights Democratic Party in 1948 and called the 1954 *Brown v. Board of Education* decision unconstitutional, immoral, illegal, and outrageous. He asserted that the National Association for the Advancement of Colored People was under Communist influence or infiltration, and he opposed the major civil rights bills of the 1960s.

Rivers died following surgery in Birmingham, Alabama, on December 28, 1970. The man servicemen often called their champion was buried in the St. Stephens Episcopal Churchyard in Berkeley County.

Following Congressman Rivers' death, his staffer and namesake, Mendel J. Davis was elected to finish out the unexpired term of Congressman Rivers. Davis served until he retired in 1980. Mt. Pleasant Republican Thomas Hartnett was elected to fill the open seat, becoming the first Republican to be elected to Congress in Lowcountry South Carolina.

★ ★

CHAPTER 5

Home Rule

★ ★

In 1975, Senator Rembert Dennis co-sponsored a bill to bring South Carolina counties and municipalities in line with a federal court ruling.

Of the five forms of government allowed under the [12]South Carolina Home Rule Act, Council form, Council-Supervisor form, Council-Administrator form, Council-Manager form, and Board of Commissioners form, Berkeley County had previously been operating under a loose version of the fifth form, Board of Commissioners.

Hanahan's new mayor, Earl Copeland, had been elected by write-in ballot in September 1975. When Senator Dennis announced two public hearings leading up to a county referendum for determining Berkeley County's form of government, and after studying the available forms to choose from under the new law, Mayor Copeland

---

12 Appendix B – South Carolina Home Rule Act of 1975, Chapter 9

Council members look on as newly elected Mayor Earl Copeland is sworn into office by City Judge Lester F. Bevil. Left to right are John R. Reeder, Marion T. Dudley, Dorothy C. Cease, Copeland, Bevil, Ralph D. Proper, Mary Lou Strickland, and Edmund L. Hester.

and Mayor Jim Richards of Goose Creek issued a joint press release. In it they announced that they would be supporting the Council Administrator form.

One of the responses to the press release was from Charleston's Channel 2 television. Their reporter, Red Evans, contacted Mayor Copeland and asked if he would agree to be interviewed. In the interview Evans asked why he had chosen the Council-Administrator form to support.

Mayor Copeland said he felt that an elected county council hiring a well-qualified administrator would be best for the citizens. Reporter Evans said that he understood that Senator Dennis was supporting the Board of Commissioners form. To which the mayor responded that Senator Dennis, who had introduced the law, included the "so called fifth form" in the law just for Berkeley County, but that it was a farce, to allow the senator to maintain control of Berkeley County.

Following the interview, the reporter interviewed Senator Dennis. That night when the interview was aired, Senator Dennis was visibly upset, and responded that "Mayor Copeland nor anyone else was going to tell the people of Berkeley County what kind of government Berkeley County will adopt."

Hearing In Moncks C.

The first of two public hearings on home rule in Berkeley County will be held tonight.

The hearing, scheduled for 7:30 p.m. at the courthouse in Moncks Corner, will focus on the five forms of government which counties may adopt under the Home Rule Act.

The second meeting will be Jan. 12 at 7:30 p.m. at the Goose Creek High School cafeteria.

In a statement Sunday, Mayor B. Earl Copeland of Hanahan said he is "convinced" the Council-Administrator form is the best system for the county and called the Board of Commissioners form a "farce." Copeland said the "Board of Commissioners should be only an advisory board with all administrative powers vested in the supervisor.

"With the purse strings controlled by the delegation and all administrative powers vested in one man, the elected body called the Board of Commissioners is a farce."

The News and Courier, Mon., Jan. 5, 1976 9-A
Charleston, S.C.

Dennis Reverses
Home Rule Stand

By THOMAS BENNETT *Jan '76*
Staff Reporter

MONCKS CORNER — State Sen. Rembert C. Dennis reversed his stand on home rule and spoke in favor of the council-supervisor form of county government at a public meeting here Monday night.

"I'm not going to campaign for the fifth (the present Board of Commissioners) form of government," Dennis said. "As I feel tonight about it, I would vote for form two (council-supervisor form)," he said.

Under the fifth form, the legislative delegation retains the power to approve the county budget and appoint the members of the Board of Commissioners.

Dennis claimed he had favored the fifth form because he feared that an inexperienced council might permit excessive spending and cause increased taxes.

Dennis said he now favored the council-supervisor form because he wants Berkeley County to be administered by an elected local official rather than a hired manager or administrator.

"I'm going to vote for the form that makes the man responsible for administering the county directly responsible to the people," he said.

A referendum on home rule had been scheduled for Feb. 10, 21 days after a scheduled Jan. 20 referendum on a water and sewer bond issue.

Dennis denied that the schedule was made scheduled to insure a light turnout on home rule and help passage of the fifth form.

He announced that the home rule referendum has been rescheduled for the second Tuesday in March. The three other members of the Berkeley delegation, Reps. Linwood Helmly, William C. Stanley and B.J. Gordon denied conspiring to push the fifth form.

Approximately 250 persons packed into the Berkeley County Courthouse for the first of two public meetings on home rule.

Russell B. Shetterly, Executive Director for the S.C. Association of Counties explained the five forms of county government and answered numerous questions from the audience.

Another public meeting is scheduled at 7:30 p.m. Jan. 12 at Goose Creek High School.

Initially Senator Dennis had said that he favored the Supervisor-Board of Commissioners form because it was closest to that under which the county had been operating. After the publicity that the controversy generated in print and on TV, Senator Dennis saw that he was on the wrong side of this issue. The so-called "fifth form" was exposed for just what it was, a plan for the senator to maintain control of Berkeley County government.

In the first referendum held March 9, 1976, the vote was a virtual tie and required a runoff vote. By that time, Senator Dennis had changed to backing Form 2, Council-Supervisor. Former Board of Commissioners Chairman Bobby Gore, who, like Copeland and Goose Creek Mayor Richards, and others, had achieved their goal in opposing the 5th Form. Form 2, Supervisor-Council passed in the second referendum two weeks later.

That was the first time in memory that Senator Dennis had not gotten what he set out to do. Leaders from the south end of Berkeley County had forcefully made a case against the form of government that "The Senator" had every intention to get passed. That was a chink in the armor of the old guard.

Berkeley Voters To Try Again

By STEVE MATHIS
Evening Post Staff Writer

Berkeley County voters will try again Tuesday to chose the form of government under which the county will operate as outlined in Home Rule legislation.

In the first referendum on March 9, voters split almost evenly between Form 2, the council-supervisor form, and Form 3, the council-administrator form.

Little has changed insofar as politicking for one form or the other goes.

Dr. David G. Cork formerly a Berkeley County commissioner, is leading a faction which supports Form 3 while Sen. Rembert Dennis, who took his first public role in the matter Wednesday, is leading the faction which supports Form 2.

Dennis signed an open letter which, in effect, said that if Berkeley County chooses Form 3, the county government will be dominated by the metropolitan areas in the southern part of the county.

Cork said, though, that Dennis and other county officials are concerned that they will lose their base of influence over county affairs if voters choose a powerful council and professional administrator.

Another question has arisen as to whether the runoff referendum constitutes a separate election or if it is an off-shoot of the first.

About 120 residents of Hanahan and Goose Creek were registered to vote on Feb. 9 but were ineligible for the March 9 referendum because of the 30-day waiting period after voter registration required by state law.

Former Goose Creek mayor Malvin Mann said today that he considers the second referendum a "whole new ballgame" and one in which persons ineligible for the first election could vote.

★ ★

CHAPTER 6

Early Challenges

★ ★

In 1985, when Peggy Dufek and Wanda Floyd, two ladies who were
members of Berkeley County Republican Women's Club, visited Earl
Copeland, he told them that if he were to agree to run for the position
of Berkeley County Republican Party Chairman, there were two things
about which he would insist. First, that the party members would be
ready to roll up their sleeves and get to work. He had no idea how they
would take the second condition.....that the Republican Party would
be open to anyone, regardless of race or religion, as long as he/she believes in the Republican philosophy of conservative government, both
economically and socially.

Prior to that time the local party had the reputation of having a
coffee-club mentality where they would meet once a month, talk about
politics, lamenting the fact that the Democrats still had a strangle hold
on Berkeley County and South Carolina and then adjourn until the

next meeting. After his election loss in a Democrat primary in June 1978 for a county council seat, he learned a valuable lesson about the importance of aligning with the political party with which one's values are more aligned. In 1980, he had written a letter to the local papers declaring his alignment with the Republican Party and his support for Ronald Reagan for President.

At the Berkeley County Republican Convention in March 1986 Copeland was elected Chairman.

Former Hanahan mayor to lead Berkeley GOP

Former Hanahan mayor Earl Copeland is the new Berkeley County Republican Party chairman.

Copeland will lead the party for the next two years.

Other officials elected recently were:

Merrill A. Cox, convention president; Judith K. Spooner, county representative on the state executive committee; Charles Snyder, 1st vice chairman; Wade Arnette, 2nd vice chairman; Becky Page, secretary; and Charles Schuster, treasurer.

Also elected were delegates and alternates to the 1st and 6th congressional district conventions and the state convention. The combined 1st and 6th district delegations will make up Berkeley County's state delegation, Cox said.

First district delegates are: Earl Copeland, Judith Spooner, Charles Snyder, Becky Page, Joanne Wenger, William Doar, Henry E. Brown Jr., Charles Rhodes, Peggy Dufek and Ruby Mitchell.

Sixth district delegates are David Dennis, J.B. Hood, John Trout, DeAnna Trout, Wade Arnette, James Lusk, Howard Kemp and Doris Schurlknight.

Immediately after his election in March 1986, Berkeley County Republican Executive Committee went to work setting goals. The GOP primary election of 1986 was in June. The new party leaders had virtually no time to prepare for the upcoming 1986 election cycle.

Right off, Chairman Copeland saw a need to change that situation in the future. New party officers taking office had just three months before a primary, which was followed just four months later by the general election, was not a good position in which to be.

The newly reactivated Republican Executive Committee was excited to begin serious work to change the political landscape in Berkeley County. Chairman Copeland decided that the best way to begin was to "come out of hiding and take the fight to the Democrats" that had controlled the county for so long. His first move was to hold their monthly meetings at Berkeley Restaurant, a place where almost every office holder and their close allies ate lunch or dinner.

He secured a room for their first meeting and asked the committee members to meet in the parking lot before going in together. As they marched into the restaurant, everyone there noticed the large group with Mr. Copeland. Many knew him from his time as mayor of Hanahan. He went through the dining room shaking hands and greeting people.

One diner asked him what was going on. He introduced the group as the Berkeley County Republican Executive Committee and told him that they would be holding their meetings there. As the committee was made up of people from voting precincts throughout the county, a few members were known to some diners.

That was long before state legislation was passed requiring the state to conduct political primaries in South Carolina. Prior to that, each party funded and ran their own primary and manned the precinct polls with volunteer workers. The new Berkeley GOP team muddled through the 1986 election, learning some valuable lessons in the process.

With the 1988 national election up next, Copeland found that many others at the 1986 GOP State Convention felt the same as he did about the timing of South Carolina voter precinct reorganization and primaries. The leaders of the 1986 State GOP Convention introduced new rules to accomplish precinct reorganization, along with county and state conventions, in off years, allowing new officers time to prepare for the 1988 election. That decision was within the admissible actions of the South Carolina Republican Party.

In 1986, when Chairman Copeland was first elected, he and the Dorchester County chairman, Stan Archenhold, met to discuss how to grow GOP participation in their two counties. In the discussion they realized that the party was structured only around meeting the requirements of the state law which governs all political parties. One thing that was clearly missing was how party members could gather on a regular basis to socialize and get to know each other on a personal basis. They came up with the idea of a joint monthly Republican breakfast.

For a few years they met monthly for a joint breakfast at the Holiday Inn hotel near I-26 exit 199, and right at the Berkeley/Dorchester county-line. They invited interesting speakers who spoke on issues relevant to its members. After a time, Dorchester's GOP leadership decided to hold their own elsewhere. One of our Berkeley members, former Goose Creek mayor, Malvin Mann, recommended that Berkeley County GOP move its monthly breakfast to the American Legion Post 166 in Goose Creek. The post volunteers cook a delicious breakfast, and the proceeds go to assisting the Legion in their many projects.

The monthly GOP Breakfast has been held at that site for over thirty years. It has grown exponentially over the years, with crowds now ranging from fifty to over a hundred attendees. It has hosted GOP officeholders and candidates from national to the local scene, as well as other speakers from whom membership think they would like to hear.

The 1987 South Carolina party reorganization brought a lot of unexpected activity. National televangelist, Pat Robertson, was preparing to run for President in 1988. He had formed a national grassroots organization, Christian Coalition, to work toward supporting candidates who shared the Christian viewpoint. One of his chief Chrisitan Coalition leaders was Berkeley County's Roberta Combs, a Hanahan resident. Roberta would go on to become National Chairman of the organization.

When Chairman Copeland was mayor of Hanahan, he got to know Andy and Roberta Combs, developer of Otranto Subdivision, and worked with them on a range of issues. At the Berkeley County reorganization, a heavy contingent of Christian Coalition supporters showed up for the precinct meetings and were instrumental in electing many precinct officers in the Hanahan and Goose Creek areas, and numerous others beyond Goose Creek. At first, many of the old party faithful resented the newcomers. A couple of them remarked to the Chairman that "they would be a flash in the pan and probably wouldn't last long." However, that was not the case.

Copeland was reelected at the 1987 Berkeley County GOP Convention. Andy Combs was elected to represent Berkeley on the GOP State Executive Committee. Under the new state rules, each county party chairman was also a non-voting member of the State Committee. There were several new members of the County Executive Committee, including some of the folk associated with the Christian

Coalition. After a bumpy start the two groups got to know each other better.

At the first Executive Committee meeting following the 1987 reorganization, Chairman Copeland reminded the participants that they all had one job; that was to focus on working to elect Republicans. If they did that, everything else would work out. The committee really had some talented and dedicated people. Two new committee members mentioned here were in that first meeting.

State Senator Larry Grooms

Larry Grooms represented the Bonneau precinct. He was the owner of two convenience stores in upper Berkeley County. Larry immediately proved himself to be levelheaded, personable, and reliable. Being a small businessman, he also had people skills and really helped to build trust between the two groups. Ten years later, in 1997, Larry ran for, and was elected, to the state senate. In 2007, he became Chairman of the Senate Transportation Committee.

Another new committee person who was elected to the Executive Committee in 1987 was a young navy wife and Florida native, Adrian Wright who represented one of the Westview School precincts. Adrian was a delightful, bright black woman. She stated that she had grown up in a Republican household and her parents were members of the Florida Republican Party. She was warmly received by the group. At the county convention most of the new officers were elected as delegates to the 1987 State GOP Convention.

At the 1987 state convention members of the Berkeley County GOP delegation met South Carolina's new governor, Carroll A. Campbell, Jr., the convention keynote speaker. The governor was impressed with Berkeley delegate Adrian Wright. He gave her a business card and told her to call him. It was later learned that he offered her the job of Director of the Governor's Office of Minority Affairs. Before long we lost Adrian to bigger things. After a couple of years in that job she was hired by the multinational defense contractor, Fluor-Daniels, as their Director of Minority Affairs and moved to their headquarters in Indianapolis, Indiana.

Following the political changes experienced in Berkeley County in the mid-1970s, Senator Dennis' political clout continued into the 1980s. Although two Republican members of County Council were elected in 1980, Judy Spooner in Hanahan, and Merrill Cox in Goose Creek, Democrats maintained solid control of County Council. But the old guard was on notice that change was in the air.

CHAPTER 7

Henry E. Brown, Jr.: Catalyst for Change

Henry Edward Brown, Jr.

Henry E. Brown, Jr. is a Berkeley County native who grew up on his family's farm in the Cordsville area outside Moncks Corner. He had worked at the Charleston Naval Shipyard where he was in the fledgling computer division. He later was hired by Piggly Wiggly Carolina in their computer department, rising to vice president.

He had a yearning for public service. He sought and was appointed as a member of the Hanahan Planning Board. In 1980, he was elected to Hanahan City Council.

State House

In 1985 during his second term on city council, Councilman Brown ran for and was elected to an unexpired term of District 99 of the South Carolina House of Representatives. There, he had a greater ability to influence events in his beloved Berkeley County. As he intended to devote his total energy to public service, he retired from Piggly Wiggly.

Brown was well known throughout Berkeley County, thus Chairman Copeland called upon him to assist in recruiting the best qualified people for elective office.

Henry E. Brown, Jr. working at his beloved 1500 acre farm adjacent to Francis Marion National Forest at Cordsville.

State Rep. Henry Brown flanked by Congressman Arthur Ravenel and Berkeley County Councilman Bob Call

Representative Brown was appointed to the South Carolina House Ways and Means Committee in 1989, and later became ranking member, as the House was controlled by Democrats. However, he built trust among his peers on the committee, both Democrat and Republican.

Outgoing Governor Carroll Campbell and Incoming Governor David Beasley with House Ways and Means Chairman Henry E. Brown, Jr. 1994

House Leadership

In the 1994 general election, Republicans became the majority party in the State House of Representatives. As ranking member, Henry became Chairman of that powerful committee. As chairman he automatically became a member of the five member State Budget and Control Board (BCB) which is chaired by the governor.

Brown to head state Ways and Means Committee

Representative Henry E. Brown, Jr., (R) Berkeley, was elected Chairman of the Ways and Means Committee by acclamation on Wednesday, December 7, during the House of Representatives' recent organizational session. In his opening remarks, Representative Brown thanked the members for their support and indicated his desire for all the Committee members to work together to respond to the voters mandate of November 8.

"I see this vote as an attack on 'business as usual' and a demand for a new, responsible and effective government....I would like for the continued effort to include all agencies in Total Quality Management and in implementing zero-based budgeting," Brown said.

The 25 member Committee is responsible for annually preparing the state's appropriation bill and handling all legislation referred to the House which affects tax laws and appropriations.

Representative Brown, the first Republican Chairman of the Ways and Means Committee in over a 100 years, has served 10 years in the House, and the last six on the House budget committee.

The House Republican leadership has identified sentencing and welfare reform, safe schools, and property tax relief among its priorities for the 1995 session. Representative Brown also noted his desire to work closely with the Governor and his Executive Budget, which will be submitted to the Legislature when it returns in January.

For Representative Brown's acceptance speech, see page 2A.

Rep. Henry E. Brown

Mr. Chairman
PTA president rises to powerful state post

By SID GAULDEN
Of The Post and Courier staff

COLUMBIA — The new chairman of the powerful Ways and Means Committee in the S.C. House of Representatives, Lanahan's soft-spoken Henry Brown, isn't a flamboyant, flashy legislator, nor is he well-versed in the Machiavellian machinations of internal politics.

A former PTA president, the 59-year-old Brown rose to one of the most powerful posts in the House

on a record of work and not for papering the House with hundreds of legislative proposals designed to garner publicity.

One of four children, Brown was born in Lee County. His late father, a Charleston Naval Shipyard employee, moved the family back to Berkeley County when Brown was a year old.

His childhood was spent on a small farm in Cordesville where his father raised livestock in addition to working at the shipyard.

Now, after 9½ years of low-key, behind the scenes work, Brown has been elevated to a high profile post that expands his constituency from the 27,000 people in House District 99 to the 3.5 million in the state.

In November, the Board of Economic Advisers predicted the state's economy would generate an additional $206 million in revenue this year. That may sound like a lot, but a fourth of that has to come

off the top to go into a reserve fund. Then there is another $160 million which has to be spent on items out of last year's budget, including paying the recurring costs for items which were funded with so-called one-time money.

"So, we really don't have any new money," Brown said in a recent interview. "We haven't addressed things like employees' pay, or any new programs, such as property tax reform."

Brown said there would be some form of property tax relief in the 1995-96 budget, along with some plans for additional governmental restructuring. But the final package is six months worth of negotiations away.

And Brown isn't overly fond of the idea of increasing the state's sales tax by a penny. "It's not as simple as replacing dollar for dollar, other factors are involved," he noted. The major goal this year is to regain the state's Triple A bond rating, which allows the state to issue bonds at a cheaper rate than can be done currently.

In an effort to make the best use of all 25 members of the Ways and Means Committee, Brown has revamped the subcommittee process. With 14 subcommittees now in place, Brown has broken the budgeting process down further than it has ever been.

"The purpose of that is not only to try to fund the agencies, but to

try to offer some direction to the agencies, to try to make the agencies more responsive and more effective."

At the same time, committee staffers are trying to chart a 20-year cycle to see if government is growing faster than personal income or faster than the Gross National Product.

"We recognize that when a program begins, it starts off without a termination date. We will look for some of those programs that have outlived their purpose," Brown said.

"We're probably going to be accused of stepping on some folks' toes because we're going to want them to justify their existence. I don't think we can simply continue a program just because somebody thinks it's a good thing.

"You've got both sides. This group that wants to be absolutely sure that we don't add anymore fees or charges and then we've got these other groups that want more and more money. It's going to be a tough decision time. But I think the people back on Nov. 8 spoke, saying 'We don't want any more government, we've got more government than we can afford.'

"I think you're going to see a different attitude toward government," Brown said.

Brown said he would support a Supplemental Appropriations Bill this year to pay for the start of the extensive State House renovations and to open a prison.

"We've got a prison in Ridgeland that is sitting there empty — a $30 million capital outlay that we bonded and are paying interest on that we're not using," Brown said. A portion of the supplemental appropriation will go toward the process of opening that prison in July, not in 1996.

A graduate of Berkeley High School. Brown took night classes at The Citadel and what was then Baptist College, while working for Piggly Wiggly as head of the firm's computer operations.

His 27 years at Piggly Wiggly shaped Brown's business principles and the conservative nature of his family and community buttressed his political conservatism. Brown also was an early and ardent supporter of Gov.-elect David Beasley.

All of that served to place Brown in a position to assume the Ways and Means chairmanship.

"I recognized that my business background would lend itself to that, but politics and reality don't cross paths very often. I think the opportunity just happened."

Driven by what he saw as a need for better government. Brown said he was willing to give politics a try in 1981.

"I've heard all my life about the crooked politicians and lack of responsiveness. I just felt like I could offer my services. The business principles and the conservative principles that have been part of my lifestyle. if I could somehow merge that into the political process. I would hope that this would make a better government. a more responsive government."

Brown. married for 39 years and the father of three children. ran for a seat on the Hanahan City Council in 1981 and was elected to fill the unexpired term of a departing council member. Prior to that he had served on the city's Planning Commission.

In 1985, the same set of circumstances opened the door for his run for the House. Rep. Francis Archibald decided to bow out of politics midway through a term.

"When Archibald resigned. some folks called and said why don't you run for that seat?" Brown talked with Piggly Wiggly officials, who readily agreed to give him the leeway to run for office.

"It was an open slot. I had no notion of every getting involved full-time in politics. I was working at Piggly Wiggly. I had a good job and I was also involved in Lowcountry Investment to help generate store operators. After I got elected, I recognized that it was full-time commitment. So. I just felt like that I would have been playing games with the company if I decided I would go back and work two days a week (for Piggly Wiggly)," said Brown.

With that decision made — it was an amiable parting — Brown became a full-time legislator, and now is in a position to put his conservative stamp on the state's budgetary process.

By requirement of the State Constitution, the House of Representatives must originate all spending bills in the General Assembly. The chairman of Ways and Means, controls the flow of financial legislation and thus the governor heavily depends on that person to assist in getting his/her agenda passed.

S. C. Legislative Budget Reconciliation Committee

The five-member Budget and Control Board is composed of the governor, as chairman, with the House Ways and Means Committee chairman, the Senate Finance Committee chairman, the State Treasurer and State Comptroller General, and is itself an executive agency. The BCB is responsible for broad policy over most other state agencies.

House Ways and Means Chairman Henry Brown, a Berkeley County Republican, has asked state agencies to cut their budgets by 5 percent. 'If you've got lots of money to spend,' he says, explaining the request, 'you spend lots of money.'

Chairman Brown became one of the two most powerful elected officials in South Carolina, the other being the governor. With his background and knowledge in the field of computers, Chairman Brown saw an opportunity to bring order to the chaos of computerization in South Carolina's government agencies.

Prior to his intervention, each agency purchased its own computers, and none of them communicated with those of their sister agencies. He developed a plan to standardize purchase and maintenance of all state government computers and software which saved millions of dollars and improved efficiency to a level that was never before realized in South Carolina.

Saving the. state millions

Charleston Post & Courier . 1/20/9?

A little-noticed budget proviso two years ago requested a broad review of state computer operations that, based on a recent recommendation to the Legislature, could save taxpayers as much as $30 million over a 16-year span. The proposal from the State Budget and Control Board demonstrates the ongoing need for streamlining state operations.

The study was sought by Rep. Henry Brown, R-Hanahan, after the Ways and Means Committee that he chairs was presented with numerous budget requests by state agencies for computer equipment and upgrades. He says the volume and variety of requests indicated that the state didn't have a handle on its data processing costs.

A review revealed the existence of 11 data processing divisions with little integration in equipment or capacity for the exchange of information among state agencies. The new centralized system, recommended by the Budget and Control Board staff, will provide for both, with a sizable reduction in staff. Rep. Brown says the program will take four years to implement and that the anticipated staff reduction of 100 can be accomplished during that time through attrition.

The proposal demonstrates the savings that are available through inter-agency integration of staff and equipment, when appropriate. A statewide performance audit of state government that will begin this year is expected to address that kind of issue in greater detail. Meanwhile, Rep. Brown should to be recognized for maintaining a businessman's eye on the budget for an economy that ultimately should save taxpayers millions.

The Charleston Post and Courier editorial here was sent to Chairman Brown by Buck Limehouse, Chairman of the South Carolina Department of Transportation, signaling his complete support of the plan.

SCDOT

**South Carolina
Department of Transportation
Commission**

8 Cumberland Street
Charleston, South Carolina 29401

H. B. Limehouse
Chairman
SCDOT Commission

January 27, 1997

Honorable Henry Brown, Chairman
Committee on Ways and Means
SC House of Representatives
Post Office Box 11867
Columbia, South Carolina 29211

Dear Henry:

Attached is a good editorial which recently ran in the Post
and Courier regarding a review of the state's computer
operations. Please be assured of the Department of
Transportations full cooperation in this matter.

I hope that you will continue to keep up your good work on
behalf of the people of South Carolina. If I can ever be of
service to you, please let me know.

Sincerely,

Buck .

H.B. Limehouse

HBL/gd

AN EQUAL OPPORTUNITY/
AFFIRMATIVE ACTION EMPLOYER

NEWS RELEASE
South Carolina Department of Revenue
Public Affairs Office
Danny Brazell, Assist. Public Affairs Director

Phone (803) 737-9864
Fax (803) 737-9881

FOR IMMEDIATE RELEASE
March 18, 1996

**STATE REPRESENTATIVE HENRY BROWN
RECEIVES DEPARTMENT OF REVENUE AWARD**

Berkeley County State Representative Henry E. Brown, Jr., of Hanahan was recently honored for his many years of public service when South Carolina Department of Revenue Director Burnet R. Maybank, III presented him with the agency's *Director's Award for Lifetime Public Service.*

Rep. Brown, chairman of the House Ways and Means Committee, received the SCDOR award because of his devotion and diligence in representing his Berkeley County constituents in legislative matters. The DCR presents the award to individuals whom the agency feels have provided exceptional public service to South Carolina citizens.

"The Department of Revenue salutes your career of dedicated service to Berkeley County and the State of South Carolina," Maybank said in presenting the award to Rep. Brown in a ceremony held last week.

Rep. Brown has been a member of the South Carolina House of Representatives since 1985. He is a retired executive with Piggly Wiggly Carolina, Inc.

During his sixteen years as a member of the South Carolina House of Representatives, Representative Brown received many awards for his leadership and vigilance in overseeing spending of tax money received from his constituents. He served in that capacity until 1999, when he resigned the chairmanship to have more time to pursue another goal.

Congress

After Congressman Mark Sanford announced that he would not seek a fourth term, Henry decided to make a run for the open South Carolina First Congressional District seat.

He invited his friend and former Berkeley County Republican Chairman, Earl Copeland, to lunch with his son, Jimmy, and himself, to discuss his decision. Copeland was stunned that he would give up his powerful position in the State Legislature, to become a 65-year-old freshman in congress. When Copeland asked him about that prospect, he simply said "I believe I can make a difference".

Copeland reminded him that local real estate developer Harry B. "Buck" Limehouse had already announced that he was running as a Republican and that he would spend a million dollars to win that seat. Copeland said to him that he, Mr. Brown, would have to have one heck of a grassroots organization to beat that kind of money. Representative Brown told him, "that's where you come in".

He informed Copeland that his top priority in Congress would be to see that "our forgotten veterans are better cared for than they currently are". He asked Copeland to organize a large group of campaign volunteers including local veterans. The first person he was to recruit was Brown's friend from their youth, Clarence "Mac" McGee who lives in St. Stephen.

Earl Copeland, Congressman Henry Brown, Mac McGee

Mac was a retired Sergeant Major of the Eighty Second Airborne Division and a former commander of the South Carolina department of American Legion, who was currently Berkeley County's Veterans Service Officer. He dealt daily with literally dozens of veterans. McGee and Copeland immediately began to lay out a plan to reach out to the veteran community in the First Congressional District. He also put together a ground level campaign team, people with whom he had worked in Berkeley and other surrounding counties in the past decade.

In March 2000, Brown filed to run for the open seat of the First Congressional District. The Republican field was crowded, with six candidates filing for the upcoming primary.

In the Republican Primary, his main opposition was a well-known Charleston businessman, Buck Limehouse. Mr. Limehouse was quoted as saying that he would spend one million dollars to win the seat, and he was true to his word. However, Representative Brown had a fantastic grassroots organization in place. The election wound up with the top two vote-getters, Brown with 44% and Limehouse with 34%. Since neither candidate received the necessary 50% plus one vote, a runoff was required.

The ensuing two weeks before the runoff primary, Mr. Limehouse's campaign mailed out several expensive negative hit pieces against Brown. But Brown had a solid reputation of honest dealings among the citizens of the Lowcountry. The final vote tally showed that Brown won the runoff by a 10% margin.

Congressman Brown Being Sworn In by U. S. House of Representatives Speaker Dennis Hastart

During the campaign Brown had said that our military and veterans would be his main priority. In his first term as congressman he sought and won a seat on the House Veterans Affairs Committee. In his second term, Congressman Brown was appointed chairman of the U. S. House Veterans Health Subcommittee. He served five terms before retiring from Congress in January 2011.

Congressman Henry Brown greeting President George Bush at Charleston Air Force Base, South Carolina

Congressman Henry Brown's political career and public service spanned five decades. He was awarded South Carolina's highest service award, Order of the Palmetto, in 2000. He received five Honorary Doctorate degrees; The Citadel, College of Charleston, Medical University of South Carolina, Coastal Carolina University and Charleston Southern University.

★ ★

CHAPTER 8

Journey to Fulfill an Impossible Dream

★ ★

In 1986 and 1987 the Berkeley County Republican Executive Committee embarked on a journey to do what many in Berkeley thought was an impossible dream....to set a new course in Berkeley County politics. The first election in which any positive change could be made was the upcoming 1988 General Election.

After discussing their goals for several weeks, the committee made a conscious decision not to try to fill every seat up for election in that cycle, but rather to initially target seats for which they were able to recruit the best candidates and for which they had a realistic chance of winning.

In the upcoming 1988 election cycle, they were able to identify one such seat. The long-time county auditor, Bill Watts, announced that he was retiring. That presented an open seat. The way the election cycle is structured in Berkeley County, 1988 was the year with the least county-wide offices up for election. Only the county auditor and county treasurer were up for grabs. The county GOP Executive Committee decided to target the open Auditor seat.

In the case of the auditor's office, Henry advised Republican leadership that his first cousin, Janet Brown Ware, worked in that office for a few years, was very competent and would make an excellent Auditor. He introduced Chairman Copeland to her.

As Mr. Copeland was also a member of the state Republican executive committee, he asked newly elected state party chairman Van Hipp to come to Berkeley County to meet with Mrs. Ware. The meeting was held but it took a bit of convincing her to run. After consulting with her father, Gamewell Brown, who was a well-known and well-respected man in Berkeley County, ultimately, she made the decision to do it.

When the word got out that Janet was going to run as a Republican candidate, retiring Auditor Bill Watts was not pleased to say the least. He had hand-picked his deputy auditor to fill that seat. What made it difficult was that she and Janet were good friends. Chairman Copeland was visiting the county office building shortly afterward, when by chance he ran into the auditor in the hallway. Mr. Watts was cordial enough but asked Mr. Copeland why he would embarrass that young lady, since she didn't stand a chance of being elected.

Berkeley County Auditor Janet Brown (Ware) Jurosko

Soon afterward, another member of the auditor's staff, Delilah Morris, was in line at a grocery store and was overheard telling a friend that she was going to support Janet. The word got back to the auditor. He called Mrs. Morris into his office and fired her. She told Janet what happened, and Janet called Chairman Copeland. He immediately filed a complaint with the South Carolina Labor Department. The agency assigned an investigator, Herbert Fielding, to the case.

State Labor Department Finds Firing Of Clerk Unjustified

By CLAIRE POOSER
Post-Courier Reporter

An investigation by the state Department of Labor concluded that the Aug. 12 firing of a clerk in the Berkeley County auditor's office was politically motivated, the clerk, Delilah Morris, said Monday.

"There's no justification to support my termination," Mrs. Morris said Labor Department officials told her. "It's due to partisan politics ... I knew it all along."

The investigation ended Friday, department spokesman James Knight said. He confirmed that the department found the dismissal was not justified. However, because the matter involved personnel, the department considered it confidential and wouldn't give details, Knight said.

The Labor Department has the authority to investigate an employ-

ee's complaint and to make a recommendation, Knight said. The recommendation carries no weight of law.

Mrs. Morris wrote to the department in September, asking that it investigate her dismissal. The case was assigned Sept. 9 to Herbert S. Fielding, labor conciliator for the Charleston region.

Mrs. Morris said she'll fight to get her job back. She began working in the office March 28.

Berkeley County Auditor William A. Watts wouldn't comment on the investigation. County Attorney Austin J. Tothacer Jr. also declined comment, "since we haven't been advised of the Labor Department's determination."

Watts told The Evening Post in September that the firing had noth-

ing to do with politics. An Aug. [...] letter from Watts to County Perso[...] nel Director Bryan Sorenson s[...] that Mrs. Morris was too sl[...] made errors and had improved o[...] slightly during a four-month peri[...]

She said she was fired because [...] was too friendly with co-worker [...] net B. Ware, the Republican can[...] date for auditor. Mrs. Morr[...] supervisor, June B. Forte, is the [...] partment's deputy auditor and [...] Democratic nominee for the au[...] tor's seat.

Independent

Wednesday, November 9, 1988

Two Sections/22 Pages/25 Cents

School sight of
formal wedding...
Page 1B

Auditor clerk firing ruled political

Labor Dept. states Morris fired from Auditor's office for political reasons

By H. Allen Morris

After completing an investigation into the firing of Delilah Platt Morris by Berkeley County Auditor William A. Watts, the S. C. Dept. of Labor has determined Mrs. Morris' firing was due to her participation in a partisan political campaign.

Mrs. Morris was fired by Watts on August 15 citing she was inefficient and incompetent in her temporary job. Mrs. Morris countered she had previously been told by Auditor Watts she was doing a good job and was not fired until after she befriended Janet Ware, the Republican candidate for Auditor. Auditor Watts openly supported Democratic candidate June Brown Forte, his deputy auditor.

Herbert S. Fielding, a Labor Conciliator, Division of Labor Management Services for the S.C. Dept. of Labor, said from his Charleston home on Monday evening, "My investigation, which was completed last Friday, showed there was no justification to support the termination of Mrs. Morris by Auditor Watts I found Mrs. June Forte, his deputy as the manager for Mrs. Morris was out of the office 50 of the 100 days Mrs. Morris was supposed to have training. After being shown examples of Mrs. Morris' work I determined if she had had a prudent manager present her weak areas would have been pointed out and given an opportunity to improve. I saw nothing to convince me Mrs. Morris was terminated for anything other than for partisan political reasons. In essence what she alleged is true."

Fielding said he talked with Auditor Watts approximately

See Firing, Page 6A

Firing

From Front Page

three weeks ago and suggested Mrs. Morris be re-hired and he refused.

Fielding's letter to Mrs. Morris stated: "I have addressed these concerns with Mr. Watts and he refuses to re-employ you with his office under any circumstances. I am satisfied there is nothing more my office can do to candidate his claim because of Mr. Watt's position; therefore, I have concluded my investigation with the recommendation you seek legal counsel in this matter."

day at his office and home says he has not seen Fielding's letter and will not comment on it until he does. He further said, "I only talked with Mr. Fielding the last of September and have not seen or talked with the men about this matter since that one time." Watts said he had not been in his office Monday afternoon since he was in Goose Creek and Hanahan campaigning for Mrs. Forte.

Fielding said he not only talked with Auditor Watts but also to Bryan Sorensen, Berkeley County's Director of Employment and Austin J. Tutacher Jr., Berkeley County attorney, on more than one accession to state his position Mrs. Morris' firing was probably not justified.

Sorensen said, "This is not a fair thing to us since we have seen nothing in writing. It's a political world, especially this time of year and I'm not shocked at any of this. It's a very serious thing, County jobs have to be above political considerations."

Sorensen also said Mrs. Morris has re-applied for a county position but was not hired for whatever reason the department director chose. "We still have her application on file and I have encouraged her to apply for other jobs," Sorensen concluded.

Earl Copeland, Berkeley County Republican Party chairman, requested the investigation after Mrs. Morris' was fired.

Copeland said on Monday afternoon, "This is very definitely a victory of the individual over good ole boy politics. It was very plain to us from the beginning the whole thing was politically motivated and was one of the worst cases of political strong arm tactics I have ever seen. We want this to serve as a notice the Berkeley County Republican Party will not sit idly by while the good ole boy crowd mistreats the working men and women in the employ of our county government. We are proud Delilah Morris had the courage to stand and fight back. We applaud her victory."

Mrs. Morris said "All I want is my job. I need to work. I said all along what I said was the truth. I'll go to higher authorities to get this thing resolved."

Following the investigation, the agency found that the firing was political and strongly recommended that the Berkeley County auditor rehire her with all back pay. With the publicity surrounding that case on TV and the newspapers, and the publicity given it in the Republican mailouts, Janet handily won the election making her the first Republican ever to be elected to a county-wide race in Berkeley County. She has been reelected to eight additional consecutive terms, retiring in December, 2024.

The other office that the Executive Committee decided to pursue, State House District 92, happened by chance.

State Representative Sandi Smith Wofford

Sandi Wofford, a well-known citizen activist, contacted Chairman Copeland and told him that she would be seeking that seat as a Republican. Sandi had lost a younger sister to an act of violence in a hold-up at a convenience store where she worked. The gunman shot and killed her, even though she had given him all the money.

After that tragedy, Sandi co-founded Citizens Against Violent Crime, a group that lobbied the South Carolina legislature for changes in our laws that would bring greater penalties in cases where guns were used in the commission of crimes. She got to know most of the members of the South Carolina General Assembly.

Mrs. Wofford decided that she could have a greater impact as a member of the House of Representatives. So, in 1988, she filed for the South Carolina House District 92 seat. Upon learning that Mrs. Wofford was planning to announce her candidacy for House District 92, the Republican Executive Committee decided to target that seat also. With Henry Brown now a member of the State House of Representatives, if the House District 92 seat could be flipped, it would help pave the way for future success.

Sandi was elected and joined her Republican counterpart, Henry Brown, as part of the Berkeley County legislative delegation. The Berkeley County GOP had made a dent in the previously solid-Democrat county legislative delegation.

CHAPTER 9

New State Leadership

Governor Carroll Campbell

Simultaneously with the changes occurring in Berkeley County, a big change was occurring at the state political level. South Carolina Fourth District Congressman Carroll A. Campbell had been elected as South Carolina's second Republican governor in 1986. As a young, dynamic leader, he inspired many younger citizens to get actively involved in the Republican Party.

One of those bright young people was a Walterboro native and attorney, Van D. Hipp.

State GOP Chairman Van D. Hipp

At the 1987 GOP state convention, with the backing of Christian Coalition supporters around the state, and many others, Van was elected state chairman of the South Carolina Republican Party. He was energized and dynamic. There was no doubt that Van was destined for greater things. In his acceptance speech, he threw down the challenges of future growth of the party and how Republicans could become the majority political party in South Carolina.

Berkeley GOP Chairman Copeland admired the freshness and zeal of the new state chairman. Soon afterwards, Chairman Hipp appointed Copeland as chairman of the State Republican Party Rules Committee. His influence in state Republican circles continued to grow.

In the 1988 Republican National Convention held in New Orleans, several Berkeley County Republicans were among the delegates and alternate delegates present. Among the list of speakers, two South Carolinians stood out. Governor Carroll Campbell, as always, was a crowd favorite, and Van Hipp, the only State GOP Chairman selected to speak, did South Carolina proud. It was at that convention that Chairman Hipp first got national exposure. Several years later, Van was chosen by Secretary of Defense Dick Chaney as Deputy Assistant Secretary of Defense for Reserve Affairs. Not long after the 2000 Presidential Election, following the terrorist attack on the World Trade Center and the Pentagon, Van oversaw activation of America's military reservists and National Guard in preparation for the Global War on Terror.

Wednesday, August 24, 1988

"Floor" activities, cajun food spice up GOP Convention stay

Governor, Party Chairman do S.C. delegation proud

by Earl Copeland

The 1988 G.O.P. Convention was my first national political convention. For those who have attended county and state political conventions, let me tell you that there are major differences. First of all, transportation is the biggest one. At a county or state convention, you drive to the convention site, participate in the event, maybe attend a party or reception, then you leave in your own vehicle.

At a national convention, even if you drive to the city, because of parking problems near the convention site, you must either take a cab or bus. I found out the first day that taking a cab would be financially intolerable. I opted to buy a bus pass for the five days I was there.

As with most cities during major conventions, all hotels had "special" prices - almost double their normal rates.

I found that New Orleans was a very hospitable city. The people were genuinely pleasant and helpful, not unlike our area. In fact I felt completely at home. I must confess, though, I ate too much Cajun cooking. Everything seemed to be loaded with cayenne pepper. Just imagine putting tabasco sauce on almost everything you eat.

Back to the convention itself - there were six sessions, two each on Monday

and Tuesday, one on Wednesday and one on Thursday. There are usually only two or three really lively peaks during a convention with the rest of the time taken up with routine business. What makes a national convention different is that there is always something happening on the floor if things get dull at the podium.

There were interviews of several well known figures right next to our seats including Henry Kissinger, Donald Trump, and Senator Phil Gramm (of Gramm, Ruddman, Hollings), who also made the nominating speech. Our delegation was directly in front of the CBS booth with NBC right next to it. Several times delegates turned to face Dan Rather with undisguised contempt, but mostly to get a closeup look at the many luminaries being interviewed by him or Tom Brokaw of NBC.

We in the South Carolina delegation had a couple of special periods of pride. One was the address by Governor Carroll Campbell. The second was the speech given by South Carolina Party Chairman, Van Hipp, Jr., who was the only s-ate party chairman invited to speak before the National Convention this year.

As is the case with so many things, a few "technicians" always try to control everything. It is commonly known as "staging." When

Earl Copeland, chairman, Berkeley County Republican Party

Van Hipp went backstage moments before he was scheduled to speak, he was handed a new speech that someone had prepared for him. He took one look at it and said, "this must be someone else's speech; its not mine." He was instructed to read through it and to read it from the teleprompter. As always, Van was prepared. He pulled a second copy of his own prepared speech from his pocket and proceeded. With adrenalin flowing, he delivered what I thought was one of the best speeches of

(continued on page 3-A)

CHAPTER 10

First Fruits in the Battle for Change

The election of 1988 was a sign that change was possible in Berkeley County. Voters had elected both Janet Brown Ware as the first Republican to win a county-wide seat, and also Sandi Wofford to represent the constituents of House Seat 92. With three Republican members of County Council, two Republican members of the South Carolina House of Representatives, and the Berkeley County Auditor, the county Republican Executive Committee was bolstered for the future.

The local newspapers carried stories of the change that was occurring in Berkeley County. [13]Allen Morris, publisher and editor

---

13 Appendix C – Allen Morris Editorial 'You Ain't Seen Nothing Yet"

of the Berkeley Democrat (the name was soon changed to Berkeley Independent), published an editorial that grudgingly acknowledged the election results.

He started the piece, "Now that the disgracefully nasty presidential race, and our almost nasty Auditor's race and County Council District 3 race are all over, we can relax a bit from the overwhelming political rhetoric we have been bombarded with these past six months." He continued, "Don't fool yourself, you ain't seen nothing yet if you think these races were a bit hot and dirty.......just wait until 1990".

He pontificated, "Win or lose this time around, understand there is a growing two-party system in Berkeley County now. If anyone ever doubted it before this election, Republican Chairman Earl Copeland has certainly erased all doubt. Not only is Chairman Earl a strong and focused leader of the Republican Party, he is also a self-appointed watch-dog against even the hint of Democratic Party cronyism, subterfuge or anything which has even a shadow of wrong doing."

He concluded, "Watch out, political good ole boys, Earl Republican-man is not going away. He is going to continue to circle like a Hawk over Democratic Party doings watching for miniscule cracks in their wall of legendary strength."

Republicans won both the targeted seats, plus kept the two County Council seats, with Bob Call having defeated Merrill Cox in the Republican primary and having gone on to win the District 3 seat in the general election. Jean Woods, Jr. defeated his Democrat opponent to win County Council District 1 seat in Hanahan. Additionally, Mike Rose won the State Senate District 38 Dorchester/Berkeley seat.

The Hanahan NEWS

serving Hanahan, Goose Creek and Lower Berkeley County

Two Sections—32 Pages

Volume XXX, No. 44

Wednesday, November 9, 1988

The Paper With A Community Spirit

In The News

TCC signs partnership agreement with IBM 5A
St. James Methodist to open new doors 7A
Low County Christmas Festival begins next week 12A
Ducks Unlimited banquet Monday 1B
Gators to be in playoffs 1B

County goes for Rose for Senate

Republicans win big in Berkeley County

Berkeley County residents cast their ballots yesterday for a new President and Vice-President of the United States. Vice President George Bush carried the County with 15,996 votes to 9,036 votes for Michael Dukakis. They also voted on State Senators, an Auditor, County Council seats, School Board representatives, and eight amendments to the S. C. Constitution.

Republican Arthur Ravenel was re-elected to the U.S. House of Representatives from District 1 (Berkeley, Charleston Counties) by a wide margin. He received 4575 votes while his challenger, Democrat Wheeler Tillman, received 1105 in Berkeley County.

A small portion of these votes.

Mike Rose
S.C. Senate, District 38

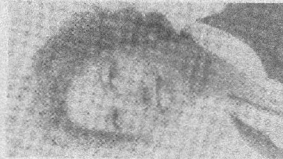

Sandi Wofford
S.C. House District 92

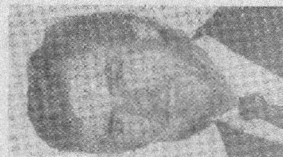

Jane Woods, Jr.
Berkeley County Council
District 3

Bob Call
Berkeley County Council
District 2

Jamet Brown Ware
Berkeley County Auditor

65

Wofford Upsets Rep. Day In House District 92 Race

By CLAIRE POOSER
and RICK NELSON
Post-Courier Reporters

Republican Sandra S. Wofford upset incumbent S.C. Rep. Fred L. Day in the House District 92 race.

District 92 includes the Goose Creek area of Berkeley County and a small portion of eastern Dorchester County in the Summerville area.

Related Story . .Page 7-B

Mrs. Wofford got 3,596 votes, according to unofficial tallies. Day received 2,336 votes. Day held the seat for three terms, and defeated Mrs. Wofford for the seat two years ago.

"The first thing I'm going to do is try to get the roads improved in Pinehill Acres, in Dorchester County, and work on the sewerage in Berkeley County," Mrs. Wofford said at a Republican victory party held at the Holiday Inn in Summerville.

Meanwhile, Democrat Robert L. Helmly, who ran unopposed for the District 37 Senate seat, will succeed Berkeley Democrat Rembert C. Dennis, who retired after 50 years of service in the General Assembly.

In the June primary, Helmly defeated Highway Commissioner Margaret Rush to become the Democratic nominee for the Sen-

See **Wofford**, Page 2-B

...Wofford

Continued From Page 1-B

ate seat.

Democrat John B. Williams ran unopposed for election to the District 100 House seat, formerly held by Helmly.

Republican Henry E. Brown Jr. ran with no opposition for the District 99 House seat he has held since 1985. And Democrat Dewitt Williams ran unopposed for the District 102 House seat he has held for three terms.

Mrs. Wofford, 36, of Summerville, is co-founder and former executive vice president of the Charleston chapter of Citizens Against Violent Crime and now serves as secretary of the organization's state board.

Helmly, 61, is president and gen-

eral manager of Home Telephone Co. He was elected to the S.C. House of Representatives in 1973 and is serving his 16th year in the Legislature.

John B. Williams, 43, is a Moncks Corner lawyer. In the Democratic primary, he defeated County Planning Administrator E. Nick Bruce.

Brown, 52, of Hanahan, is a retired vice president for Piggly Wiggly Carolina Co., Inc. He served two terms on Hanahan City Council and was a member of the Hanahan Planning Commission. In the General Assembly, Brown is a member of the House Judiciary Committee and its Criminal Law subcommittee.

Dewitt Williams, 69, of St. Stephen, considers himself a full-time legislator. He was a member of St. Stephen Town Council from 1970-79, during which he was mayor pro tempore for five years.

In the spring of 1988 at the First Congressional District GOP Convention held in Charleston, Chairman Copeland was elected as an alternate delegate to the upcoming Republican National Convention to be held in New Orleans. He was also nominated by Dorchester County Republican Chair, Annette Young, and was elected, to represent the First Congressional District as one of eight South Carolina members of the Presidential Electoral College in the upcoming presidential election.

Electors

From 1-A

The scene was repeated in ceremonies across the nation Monday. Bush and Quayle, who amassed a 40-state victory on Election Day, received more than the 270 electoral votes required for election. A final vote of 426 for Bush and 112 for Massachusetts Gov. Michael Dukakis was expected nationwide.

Checking off Bush and Quayle's names on ballots, then signing sheaves of gold-sealed legal documents under bouncing television lights, South Carolina's electors confirmed that the GOP ticket carried the state last month, winning all eight of the state's votes in the Electoral College — the 200-year-old system that actually elects presidents and vice presidents.

Wisconsin's electors, after delivering their 11 votes to Dukakis and running mate Lloyd Bentsen as planned, also voted nine-to-two to pass along to Congress some unsolicited advice. They passed a resolution urging a constitutional amendment abolishing the Electoral College system.

But that view was not held in South Carolina. "I like (the Electoral College)," said state GOP Chairman Van D. Hipp of Charleston, one of the state's two at-large electors. "It's a constitutional tradition we ought to keep."

Hipp said no South Carolinians had suggested that he refuse to cast his electoral vote for vice president-elect Quayle, but said he'd received "some nut mail" from writers in California and Washington state, asking electors across the nation not to certify Quayle.

He said all eight South Carolina electors apparently got the mailings, even though they were sworn to vote for whomever carried the state.

Besides Hipp, South Carolina's electors were: Dan Ross, at-large; Earl Copeland, 1st Congressional District; Joe Strickland, 2nd District; Walt Owens, 3rd District; Beverly Russell, 4th District; Lake High, 5th District; and Gene Beckman, 6th District.

Ginger Pinson/The State

Earl Copeland of District 1 looks over signatures

As one of eight South Carolina Presidential Electors, Chairman Copeland, as did all other electors, had two seats down front of the inauguration stage. As his wife and daughter were attending also, he stood far back in the crowd and allowed his wife and daughter to be seated.

Page 14A-THE BERKELEY INDEPENDENT, Moncks Corner, SC, February 1, 1989

Inaugural revelers-Stopping conversation to pose for a photo at the South Carolina Inaugural Ball is (R to L) Dr. Harry Lightsey, College of Charleston president, First Congressional District Rep. Arthur Ravenel, North Charleston Mayor John Bourne, his wife, Mrs. Blanche Bourne, Lisa Copeland, Mrs. Linda Copeland, Berkeley County Republican Party Chairman

The three people not identified in this photo to the right of Berkeley County Republican Chairman Earl Copeland were: Mrs. Mitzi Langdale of Hanahan, State Republican Chairman Van Hipp, and Dr. Emery Langdale.

Berkeley County represented at Presidential Inauguration

By H. Allen Morris

At 12:03 p.m., Friday, January 20, 1989 while George Walker Herbert Bush, the 41st President of the United States, took the oath of office, Berkeley Countians were among the some 140,000 persons who witnessed the impressive ceremony.

Earl Copeland, Chairman of the Berkeley County Republican Party, received a special invitation as one of South Carolina's eight Presidential Electors. He, along with his wife, Linda, and their oldest daughter, Lisa attended the official oath of office, the parade and the South Carolina Inaugural Ball.

Chairman Copeland said, "As I witnessed the ceremony I realized after two hundred years, the greatest experiment the history of human government proved once again the fantastic wisdom and foresight of our nation's founding fathers.

"The Constitutional provisions of our democratic republic still work smoothly in the peaceful transfer of power as dictated by the will of a majority of our citizens."

While in Washington Copeland said he talked with fellow Berkeley Countians Steve Jarrell who writes and takes photographs for *The Hanahan News*, Michele Combs, S. C. President of the Federation of Young Republicans, Dr. and Mrs. Emory, Charles Schuster, Karen Scott and Drew Byron who is now employed in Washington.

Also attending was Rebecca Page, former Berkeley County Republican Party Secretary who is a member of Congressman Arthur Ravenel's Washington staff.

After arriving in Washington Thursday, Jan. 19, about noon, Chairman Copeland and his family visited Congressman Ravenel's office and Senator Strom Thurmond's office.

On Inauguration Day, the Copelands began their Washington day at 8:30 that morning after driving in from Arlington, Va. where they were staying.

Copeland said, "On the way in we heard on the radio admonitions not to even think about driving into Washington. With some fast maneuvering, and a bit of luck, we probably found the only open parking space within ten blocks of the Capitol. We parked only three blocks away, right on the Mall.

"There were masses of people. The weather was pleasant until about an hour before the swearing-in when cold gusty winds began to come in. Even wearing an overcoat, the wind seemed to cut through.

"We noticed helicopters patrolling overhead and around the perimeters of the massive crowd. We could also see security agents on the tops of buildings surrounding the area. We were told over 5,000 unarmed police officers were imported from other cities for crowd control.

"As the swearing in time neared, we could feel the excitement pulsing throughout the crowd when President Reagan entered the area and was introduced. The loudest applause came when President Bush thanked former President Reagan for all he has done for America while serving as President. It was at that point the transition of power was complete."

Copeland continued, "We saw bits and pieces of the parade as we walked approximately three miles down the Mall to the Vietnam War Memorial. We found the Memorial to be a sobering experience when we found the names of two acquaintances who died in that war.

"That night our experience was crowned with our attendance at the South Carolina Inaugural Ball held at the Hotel Washington, only a block form the White House. It was very festive with great food."

Copeland concluded, "While it is an experience we shall never forget and enjoyed thoroughly, it was good to get back to Berkeley County."

CHAPTER 11

From Campaigning to Governing

Throughout 1989, the citizens of Berkeley County were following the new office holders to see if the trust they placed in them in the last election was warranted. Mrs. Ware immediately set about to find ways to improve efficiency in the Auditor's Office. She had always made friends with her peers in the County Office Building, so she was not a new personality for them to have to get used to. As the new auditor, she fitted right in.

With Henry Brown now in his second full term as State Representative, and highly regarded, not just in his House District 99, but throughout Berkeley County, Janet had an ally on the county legislative delegation. Henry's instinct about her being a great person for the job paid off. This certainly made her transition easier. Also, having three fellow Republicans on County Council helped her comfort level in dealing with the mostly Democrat county administration. Not to worry, she herself was fully competent to do the job with years of experience in that office.

★ ★

CHAPTER 12

The Work Pays Off – Planning for 1990 Elections

★ ★

With the taste of victory in the two 1988 targeted seats, the Berkeley County Republican Executive Committee set their sights on having a full slate of Republican candidates lined up for the 1990 election cycle. That meant some serious recruiting of candidates who would not only be fully qualified but would also be people whose characters were above reproach.

Once again, Chairman Copeland turned to Representative Henry Brown for help in identifying such possible candidates. The positions that would be up for election in that cycle included the top offices in county government, County Supervisor, the highest administrative official who also serves as chairman of County Council, and the office of Berkeley County Sheriff. Much earlier in the year party chairman Copeland had met with Ray Isgett, who was a security consultant for South Carolina Electric and Gas, and a former police officer. Isgett was already exploring the possibility of running for sheriff.

Other county-wide offices that would be up for election included the offices of Coroner, Clerk of Court, Probate Judge, and RMC, the office of deeds registration. All would be uphill battles against the entrenched Democrats.

★ ★

CHAPTER 13

Changing the Political Landscape

★ ★

Handling the Negative Stuff

The 1990 election cycle started with a bang and never let up until the November General Election. There was a constant flurry of activity. Aside from the hard campaigning of every Republican candidate, the Executive Committee worked very hard at raising the necessary funds for an effective and hard-hitting campaign. Everyone knew that it would be an uphill battle to unseat entrenched Democrats.

Following the June Republican primary, Chairman Copeland called a meeting of all new candidates. In the meeting, he told every candidate that he wanted each of them to focus on running very positive campaigns. He said that when anything even remotely negative came up, they were to give it to him to handle.

Chairman Copeland and a close confidant, County Councilman Bob Call, who was not up for reelection in that cycle, met every week for breakfast or lunch to map out strategy for that week. Copeland trusted Call's counsel. Much of their weekly agenda focused on the sheriff's race. There was so much negative stuff happening in the department that it was hard to know just where to start.

One of the first things to come up was when the chairman received a call from a Dorchester County deputy sheriff. The deputy informed Copeland that there was a rumor circulating that one of Berkeley's GOP candidates was using illegal drugs. Whether it was true or just someone planting the rumor to hurt someone with whom the gossiper had a beef, such a rumor would be devastating, and would harm every Republican candidate.

Copeland independently decided to call for every Republican candidate to take a drug test. He did not immediately notify the Executive Committee or the candidates. He reasoned that if the word got out, and that if it were true, the person would temporarily stop using the illegal drug. Although he realized that it may put candidates in an awkward position, he decided it was the best course of action to advise them after making a public announcement. He arranged with a lab to do the screening.

The chairman called an emergency meeting of the candidates and informed them that he had just issued a press release that every Republican candidate would take a drug test the next day. As he expected, almost every person in the meeting was highly upset. When someone asked him who would pay the $30 lab fee for each test, he responded that every candidate, and he, himself, would pay for his/her own test. It took a while for things to settle down. He explained the predicament they all faced. When they considered that, everyone agreed to participate. Every one of the candidates passed the test the next day.

Challenging Corrupt Practice

In January 1990, upon seeing a political ad by Berkeley County Probate Judge William W. "Pee Wee" Peagler, announcing his candidacy for Berkeley County Supervisor, Chairman Copeland wrote a letter to the South Carolina Supreme Court Judiciary Standards Committee Executive Secretary, Mabry Binnicker, asking that body to investigate this infraction of the high court's rules that regulate the conduct of all judges in South Carolina, whether appointed or elected.

After mailing the letter, Copeland took a copy of the letter to Probate Judge Peagler at his office. The judge greeted Copeland and Councilman Call and asked what he could do for him. Chairman Copeland handed him a copy of the letter that he had just mailed. Upon reading it, Judge Peagler became very angry and ordered him to leave his office. A few days later, Chairman Copeland received an acknowledgement from Mr. Bennicker saying they would investigate the matter.

Five months later, in June, Mr. Copeland and his wife left on a car trip to Texas to see his son and other friends who lived in Texas. Just prior to leaving, he called a press conference at the Berkeley County Office Building where he passed out a press release. In it he questioned why, after six months nothing had been done about the Peagler situation, asking if it was the "good ole boy network" protecting one of their own.

After arriving in Texas, Copeland called home and talked with his daughter. She told him that a state highway patrolman delivered a letter from the Judicial Standards Committee in person to their home, and that he was getting numerous calls from the media. He advised his daughter that he would get the package when he returned home in two weeks, and he wouldn't be calling again.

When Copeland returned home, he read the letter that directed him to call Mr. Bennicker immediately. He knew that he had struck a nerve. He called and listened as Binnicker read the riot act, telling him that he was under a gag order not to discuss the issue with anyone. He said in no uncertain terms that if he violated it, he would find himself in jail.

Shortly after finishing the conversation with Bennicker, Copeland answered a call from a Post and Courier reporter, Arlie Porter. The reporter asked why Chairman Copeland issued the press release, but then wasn't taking calls from the media. The chairman informed him "that he couldn't talk about it". The next day the reporter's article headline read "Apparently Copeland is Under a Gag Order." More good media coverage!

Copeland calls for resignation of probate judge

In a recent press conference called by B. Earl Copeland, Chairman of the Berkeley County Republican Party, the following statement was released:

"It is my belief that it is not only our collective responsibility as private citizens but also my responsibility as Republican Chairman to assure that candidates and office holders alike must represent themselves above reproach in their positions of public trust. This is especially true of public office holders. Because of the situation which exists in the office of Judge of Probate, I have today asked the Judicial Standards Commission of South Carolina to take immediate action to remove Judge Peagler from his office."

"Research of the Code of Judicial Conduct, Canon 7 A(3) clearly reveals that Judge Peagler is in violation by seeking the office of Berkeley County Supervisor, a non-judicial position, while holding the position of Judge of Probate. I have provided the Judicial Standards Commission with evidence of this misconduct," he added.

Copeland said in a letter to Peagler, "According to the commentary of Canon 7, the reason for such a rule is to insure the integrity of the office of Probate Judge by preventing even the appearance that a judge's decision might be politicaly motivated. While I don't think that you would ever use your position for personal political gain or be influenced by the political process in the adjudication of cases before you, it is not for people like us to decide because the South Carolina Supreme Court has made its position very clear. Canon 7 A(3) of the Code of Judicial Conduct states, 'a judge should resign his office when he becomes a candidate either in a party primary or in a general election for a non-judicial office'. As a member of the Judicial family you have accepted these rules and are

(continued on page 3-A)

Goose Creek - Hanahan area news conference

Judge Peagler to announce candidacy for County Supervisor

Probate Judge William W. "Pee Wee" Peagler, in a telephone release to the Hanahan News has set February 3rd for his public announcement of his intention to seek the Democratic nomination for Berkeley County Supervisor.

Peagler will oppose incumbent Johnnie T. Flynn in the June Democratic primary.

The event, directed to the residents of Hanahan - Goose Creek, will be held, according to Peagler, at the Oaks Country Club in Goose Creek beginning at 2 o'clock on Saturday, February 3rd.

The public is invited. Hors d'oeuvres will be served after the announcement.

Peagler stated that he will be running as a conservative Democrat.

Copeland calls

(continued from page 1-A)

obligated to conduct yourself accordingly."

Copeland further stated at the press conference, "Regardless of what happens in either of the upcoming contests for Supervisor or Probate Judge, I believe that the integrity of the Office of Probate Judge must be protected against any appearance of impropriety. That is an office of the people and I am satisfied to let the voters of Berkeley County decide who should fill it in the future. For now, I am convinced that Judge Peagler should not remain in this office."

Copeland questions Judicial 8/27/1990
Standards Committee
on Peagler issue

In a press release issued last week by B. Earl Copeland, chairman of the Berkeley County Republican Party, the chairman raised the question of why it has taken five months for the Judicial Standards Committee to make a decision in his call for the removal of Probate Judge "Pee Wee" Peagler from office.

In a letter dated January 28, 1990, Copeland called to the attention of the committee's executive secretary, Mabry Binnicker, his claim that Judge Peagler was in violation of Canon 7 of the Supreme Court's rules which calls for any judicial officer to resign upon becoming a candidate for a non-judicial office. Peagler became a candidate for the office of Supervisor, a non-judicial office, earlier this year.

In a letter which he received just five days after writing the committee which oversees the ethical conduct of judges in South Carolina, Copeland was informed that the committee would take up the matter in its "next meeting" and would inform him of the decision. "After waiting five months, I began to get the feeling that someone in that office was stonewalling the issue", Copeland said, "so on last Monday, June 16th, I contacted Mr. Binnicker in Columbia to find out the status. I was informed that the investigation was still going on."

Copeland said he questions if the information has been presented to the judges who sit on the Judicial Standards Committee for their consideration and disposition. "Maybe this sort of thing is why our court system is so bogged down," he quipped. "There is no earthly reason why it would take five months to get a decision on such a straight forward, clear cut violation," he said.

"The question of ethics goes much further than Peagler drawing full salary as a judge while campaign-ing full time for a non-judicial office," the chairman continued, "at the heart of this issue is the reason the Supreme Court has issued the rules of behavior in the first place." I have passed along to Mr. Binnicker that I have been told that several attorneys who practice before the Berkeley Probate Court are upset at having received a letter from Judge Peagler asking for contributions toward his campaign for Supervisor."

"If this is true, and I for one am convinced that it is, this is even a more serious violation of the judicial code of ethics since these attorneys are put in the position, if they refuse to contribute, of not being able to properly represent their clients before this probate judge for fear of reprisal in the decisions he hands down," Copeland continued.

The G.O.P. chairman said that it will surprise him if the decision is made to directly remove Peagler from office. "I truly hope that our court system has risen above good old boy politics; but if things run true to form, to keep from publicly embarrassing him, the judge will probably receive a telephone call strongly suggesting that he step down. That way he would be allowed to announce that he was voluntarily stepping down because of his 'concern for the good of the people of Berkeley County' in an attempt to make himself appear a hero instead of someone who has continued to be paid by the taxpayers in spite of judicial rules against it," he said.

Copeland said that he intends to call for public censure on the matter of the judge's letter asking for campaign contributions if it proves true. He also stated that he has received information that another more serious complaint has been filed against the probate judge which reportedly resulted in a case being transferred to another county's probate court. "We are now looking into that matter," he said. "You never know what rotten stuff is in a barrel until you pry the lid off."

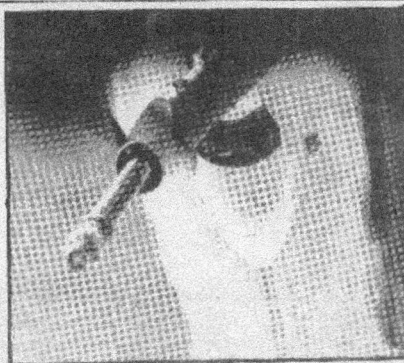

What's it?

If you were in the cockpit of an airplane at 20,000 feet and saw this contraption approaching would you believe that Star Wars had become a reality and you were about to be fired upon by an alien spacecraft and immediately begin evasion tactics? See page three for more details.

79

Major Party Switch

Solicitor Charlie Condon's Switch to the Republican Party

In 1990, a major coup took place when Democrat Nineth Circuit Solicitor Charlie Condon (representing Charleston and Berkeley Counties) announced that he was switching to the Republican Party.

THE EVENING POST

CHARLESTON, S.C., WEDNESDAY, MARCH 7, 1990

Democratic Defections Beginning To Hurt

It's been quite a week for South Carolina Republicans. They got themselves a House member, a sheriff, a county councilman and two school board members in Horry County Tuesday, not to mention a solicitor in Charleston a day earlier. Small wonder the Democratic reaction is getting more and more aggressive.

When 9th Circuit Solicitor Charles M. Condon left the fold, for example, he was called a "quitter" and his record was attacked. There was a time when Democrats were able to take the switches a little more philosophically. But that was when there seemed little chance in their lifetimes that the minority party might gain control of the Legislature and/or courthouses. Now, that prospect is no longer so remote.

While Democrats still have a comfortable edge in the Legislature, the defection by Horry Rep. Liston Barfield gives the Republicans 42 out of 124 House members. That's been a goal of sorts for the GOP since they got Carroll A. Campbell Jr. in the governor's office. If House members voted strictly along party lines, there now are enough Republicans to sustain the governor's vetoes.

Rep. Barfield brings to five the total number of House members who have switched in the last 12 months. Republicans also have snared a senator during that period. A few weeks ago, three Democratic officials in Beaufort — the treasurer, auditor and a county councilman — all became Republicans. A total of 14 officials elected at the county level have switched since last

[14]Condon and Ray Isgett, the Republican candidate for Berkeley County sheriff, were longtime friends. Isgett contacted Berkeley Republican Chairman Copeland and told him that he and Solicitor Condon had been discussing the possibility of Condon switching to the Republican Party. Isgett told Copeland that Condon had indicated that he would probably make the move if Governor Carroll Campbell would agree to come to Charleston to make the announcement. Isgett arranged for Copeland to meet with the solicitor to discuss it. The solicitor asked Copeland if he could facilitate the arrangements with the governor.

A few days later Chairman Copeland called Solicitor Condon and informed him that the governor was excited by the news and would be delighted to be with him when he made the announcement. Four years later in 1994, Charles M. Condon was elected as South Carolina Attorney General, where he served two terms before returning to Charleston to rebuild his private law practice.

[15]In June 1990, leading up to the 1990 General Election, Allen Morris, Publisher and Editor of the Berkeley Independent wrote an editorial that he titled "Is A Republican Sweep Possible?"

In it he wrote, "Be assured Republican party chairman, hawk-eyed, vociferous voiced chairman B. Earl Copeland, wasn't kidding when he said Tuesday night he believed a Republican sweep in Berkeley County is now possible in the November 6 general election, the future political focus of Berkeley County, which will carry well into this last decade before we reach the 21st century, will be sealed.........."

---

14 Appendix L – Post and Courier 1990 Editorial 'Defections' Part 2
15 Appendix D – Berkeley Independent Editorial 6/13/1990

To illustrate just how out of control the Berkeley County sheriff's department had become under Sheriff M. C. Cannon, Chairman Copeland and Councilman Bob Call decided to focus on the issues existing in the department. They learned from one of the Berkeley County deputies that there was widespread discontent among the more honest and dedicated deputies. The sheriff was content to be the head of the department but exercised little to no control over its personnel; choosing rather to let two of his lieutenants, Jim Preacher and Sidney Wrenn, run the department.

Every time someone in the media or Republican Party asked direct questions about an issue, the Chief Deputy, Jim Preacher, would run interference for the sheriff. So, Copeland and Councilman Call decided that if Mr. Preacher wanted to act the part of sheriff, he would be fair game, as a public figure, to go after the chief deputy.

In June 1990 Chairman Copeland received anonymously in the mail a copy of a federal court document signed by a federal magistrate in Charleston. There was no doubt in Copeland's mind that the document was an authentic court document. But what was not apparent was from where it had come. It stated that in 1977, Berkeley County Chief Deputy, Jim Preacher, prior to becoming a deputy sheriff, had been charged with a felony.

Copeland and Councilman Call made a trip to research the Charleston News and Couriers' archives to see if there was a story around the time of the event in 1977. They found an article that talked about an event of a break-in at a residence in the Aichele Terrace community in North Charleston where some weapons were stolen. During the investigation by North Charleston police, and because the suspect named a Berkeley County man as the 'fence' used in disposing of the weapons, the decision was made by North Charleston police to call in the feds. The article didn't name what federal agency was involved, and initially, most people thought it was the FBI.

Copeland decided to write a letter to the editors of the local weekly newspapers. In it he recited the fact that he had received the court document anonymously in the mail. Then he asked the question, was Mr. Preacher charged with a federal felony count that was plea bargained down to a misdemeanor?

A furious reaction immediately ensued. The headlines in the next edition of the Berkeley Independent screamed. "GOP Chairman Sued by Berkeley County Sheriff's Deputy".

County GOP chairman files counterclaim against Deputy Sheriff

By H. Allen Morris
Independent Editor

B. Earl Copeland, Berkeley County Republican Party Chairman, filed a counterclaim against the $250,000 libel suit of Sheriff Dept. Lt. James A. Preacher on Friday, July 20.

Copeland's counter suit states: (Preacher's) action sued upon in this case is a frivolous one within the meaning of the South Carolina code of laws and that (Copeland) is informed and believes he has been aggrieved by (Preacher's) initiation of this lawsuit...and that (Preacher)...has violated the South Carolina Frivolous Civil Proceedings Sanctions Act, and as such, is entitled to an award of attorney's fees, and court costs in his favor,

and that (Preacher's) complaint be dismissed with costs, and (Copeland) be granted judgement on his counterclaim, and for such other and further relief on as the Court may deem just and proper."

Lt. Preacher filed his suit, Thursday, June 28, citing Copeland for an alleged "libel" about Preacher, written by Copeland in the form of a letter and published in *The Berkeley Independent* and the Hanahan News in the September 6, 1989 editions.

Among the allegations listed the complaint filed by Preacher:

The suit alleges the letter Copeland wrote contained "allegations...(Preacher)...had been arrested on a serious felony charge that was reduced

by some type of plea bargain and that...(Preacher) did otherwise perjure himself on his federal employment application by not disclosing his federal conviction.

"That such statements were made by (Copeland)...with the intent to injure...(Preacher)...and his name and reputation...

"That the publication of accusations are false and defamatory words...

"That it is understood by some parties reading same article that...(Preacher)...had admitted such criminal offenses...

"That such accusations made by (Copeland)...were false and untrue and were

See SUIT...............Page 6A

SUIT
From Front Page

maliciously made...

"That...(Copeland)...knew or should have known that the statements were false and untrue.

"That...(Copeland)...published them with actual malice and hatred towards...(Preacher)...or with reckless disregard for the truth, and has otherwise harmed...(Preacher)..., his reputation in the community of which he lives and works; all to his damage in the sum of...$250,000...actual damages and for punitive damages in an appropriate amount."

Copeland's counter suit states, "The letters written by (Copeland)...are and were true, and statements were made while (Preacher) was conducting a campaign as spokesman for Sheriff M. C. Cannon. Further, the statements made...were justified by the

occasion, and were qualifiedly privileged as fair comment and criticism."

And "That (Preacher) was then a public official and a public figure and what was written and published about him was in the public interest, and (Copeland) acted in good faith, without malice, and with good and reasonable cause to believe that the contents of said statements true."

Lt. Preacher said on Sunday evening, "My suit speaks for itself. I am aware of the Frivolous Suit statute, and the burden of proof is on Mr. Copeland's attorney and Mr. Copeland.

"I am fully confident and satisfied with the system we live under. I feel like my name will be cleared, and I will be awarded the damages I am due."

Paul Gibson, a Charleston attorney representing Copeland, said, "I'm sure the suit against Mr. Copeland will be dismissed, and the Court will find in his favor."

Sheriff candidate Ray Isgett put Chairman Copeland in touch with an attorney friend, Paul Gibson, and set up a meeting with him in his North Charleston office. Mr. Gibson told Copeland to bring everything he had with him.

In the meeting, he read through the material. In the News and Courier article from 1977, attorney Gibson asked Copeland if he had learned which federal agency was involved. Copeland said that he had heard that in the past Jim Preacher had sued someone over the same issue and the case was settled out of court because that person thought the FBI was involved but could not find the records to prove it.

Attorney Gibson exclaimed "that is because it wasn't the FBI! It would have been ATF because it involved firearms." He told Copeland that he had a close friend who was a Naval Criminal Investigative Service (NCIS) agent and he worked closely with ATF on investigations. He immediately called his friend and asked him if he remembered who was agent-in-charge of ATF in South Carolina in 1977.

It turned out that his friend remembered the ATF agent's name and had remained in touch with him over the years after his retirement to his home in Oklahoma City. Gibson's NCIS friend telephoned the former ATF agent and asked him if he remembered the name Jim Preacher from his days in South Carolina. He immediately explained that not only did he remember him, what happened in that case still rankled him all those years later. He agreed to do a video deposition if Mr. Gibson were to come to Oklahoma City.

Attorney Gibson informed the Berkeley County Clerk of Court that he was going to Oklahoma City to take the deposition and asked them to officially notify Preacher's attorney so that he could be there at the deposition. Preacher's attorney did not show up for the deposition.

When Gibson returned from Oklahoma City, he notified Preacher's attorney that Mr. Copeland was ready to go to trial.

Some of the information that the former head of ATF in South Carolina provided to Attorney Gibson was that the ATF files in that case resided in the Washington DC archives. Gibson made a formal request for and received the files.

The investigation had led to the questioning and search of Mr. Preacher's vehicle and home. In the vehicle, blasting caps were found in the unlocked glove compartment. The federal agent questioned him as to why he had in his possession material that is used in the detonation of dynamite. He told them that he did some dynamiting of stumps for a developer. However, he did not have any documentation that supported his claim. The blasting caps had numbered controls printed on each cap. He was subsequently arrested for illegal possession of explosive materials.

At the time of the charges, the U. S. Attorney for South Carolina, Henry McMaster, was overseeing a major investigation of drug cartels moving illegal drugs through the state to New England via the I-95 corridor. To be able to focus on those major cases, Mr. McMaster reportedly made the decision to plea bargain many less important felony cases down to misdemeanors. The Preacher case was one of those.

A rumor had been around that Mr. Preacher felt safe from any future attempts from anyone making the information public because, his attorney had reportedly informed him that the file had been expunged. It may have been locally, but what he and his attorney had not counted on was that anyone would know to look in a federal agency archives in Washington, DC.

Preacher's attorney tried to get Copeland to publicly apologize to his client in exchange for dropping the case. With the large amount of evidence now available that showed that Chairman Copeland was, in fact, right about everything he said in the letter that he published, Attorney Gibson declined his offer. So ended the saga of the lawsuit against Chairman Copeland.

Another hot issue developed when Councilman Bob Call learned from a Berkeley deputy that the sheriff was using his deputies to work on his mountain home that was being built in North Carolina. Because it was across state lines, Copeland and Call decided to ask the FBI to investigate. When the agency indicated it was not very excited to become involved, Copeland and Call decided to make the issue public through press releases.

As all the various issues unfolded leading up to the general election of 1990, Republicans were gaining confidence that the sheriff's race was well within grasp. There were stories about the issues in several newspapers. After the Charleston Evening Post reporter started asking questions, it was learned that there was another issue involving Chief Deputy Preacher sending another deputy to serve a warrant in a county over one hundred miles from Berkeley. The result was an Evening Post Editorial on July 17, 1990. The Berkeley County Councilman mentioned in the last paragraph of the editorial was Councilman Bob Call.

THE EVENING POST

Founded Oct. 1, 1894

BARBARA S. WILLIAMS
Editor
ROBERT J. COX
Assistant Editor

MICHAEL J. BONAFIELD
Associate Editor
CHARLES R. ROWE
Associate Editor

CHARLESTON, S.C., TUESDAY, JULY 17, 1990

—— Editorials ——

Blunder In Berkeley

Is the Berkeley County Sheriff's Department willing to go the extra mile to help with something as simple as a summons on a child support case? That and more, it seems.

A sheriff's lieutenant contends he did nothing wrong by authorizing a deputy to serve a summons in another county on the ex-husband of the lieutenant's wife. Perhaps questions about the propriety of the trip would never have been raised if the summons were issued in an adjacent county. But the deputy drove a county patrol car to Chester, 150 miles from Moncks Corner.

Maybe it wasn't "illegal or unethical," as the officer contends. But it sure wasn't smart.

Lt. James A. Preacher Jr. held a press conference on Friday to defend his actions in the department's latest gaffe. He explained that the man on whom the summons was served faces a complaint from another ex-wife, and that the action was instigated by her lawyer, and not by the lieutenant's wife. Lt. Preacher points out that the lawyer has reimbursed the county for the expenses of the trip.

Lt. Preacher, however, didn't offer any substantial explanation about a policy that would allow a deputy to serve a summons in a child-support case, outside of the county. With the alleged manpower problems cited by the Sheriff's Department, it seems like deputies could be better used within the confines of Berkeley County.

Sheriff M.C. Cannon, again, has refused to comment on the matter. "He is not available to you," is the way his secretary put it. Maybe the sheriff doesn't see any problem in mixing department business and matters that could be construed as personal. He certainly didn't raise the question when deputies were charging long-distance personal calls to the county from his vacation cottage in North Carolina.

Lt. Preacher contends that the county councilman who brought the subject up only did so to embarrass the department. Too frequently, the department's own personnel does a more thorough job of that than any critic ever could.

89

[16]In a candidate forum sponsored by the Berkeley County NAACP, as reported by Charleston Evening Post political writer Arlie Porter, Sheriff M. C. Cannon and candidate Ray Isgett sparred over Berkeley County's growing drug problem. Cannon said that he was the first Berkeley County sheriff to have a narcotics unit. Isgett said that a main part of fighting the illegal drug problem is education and it should involve schools, churches and communities. Isgett also said that the sheriff's department should be held accountable for spending money confiscated through drug busts. Cannon responded that it "may jeopardize deputies or informants", as if accounting for the money from drug busts required naming which deputies and informants were responsible for the money confiscated.

[17]On November 7, 1990, Berkeley Independent editor Allen Morris wrote another editorial titled "Voters speak with loud voice". In it he stated, "It was a true contest between whether the 'Good Ole Boy' system, long a tradition in the county Democratic Party, should continue, and those who decided with a combined loud voice to turn the 'Good Ole Boy' politicians out". That is exactly the case that the Berkeley County Republican Chairman and other Republican leaders made leading up to this moment.

Those two 1990 editorials were vastly different from earlier editorials leading up to the 1988 election when Mr. Morris ridiculed Chairman Copeland and those who dared to challenge the status quo of the long-standing Berkeley County Democrat 'Good Ole Boy' system in the county. Morris went so far as to change the name of the newspaper from the Berkeley Democrat to the Berkeley Independent.

---

16 Appendix I – Evening Post Article by Arlie Porter
17 Appendix F – Berkeley Independent Editorial 11/7/1990

In an article that appeared in the [18]Charleston Post and Courier the day after the November general election, staff reporter Arlie Porter wrote, "About 70 percent of registered voters voted, a fantastic turn-out, election officer John Trout said...." Overall Republicans captured five of nine contested races.... An ecstatic Earl Copeland, chairman of the county Republican Party, said the results "were beyond our wildest dreams."

Those five contested races that Republicans captured were, Supervisor, Sheriff, Coroner, Register of Mesne Conveyances (RMC name changed to Register of Deeds in 1998) and County Council District 5. The two most important positions in the county were the top prizes, Supervisor and Sheriff.

Election Night – Rozier, Isgett, Copeland, Arnett and Forte

18 Appendix E - Charleston Post and Courier article by reporter Arlie Porter

Between the elections of 1988 and 1990, the Berkeley County Republican Party held numerous fundraising events. Chairman Copeland called State Executive Committeeman Andy Combs, and his wife Roberta, "a fundraising dynamo". They were well-known Republican activists and held several of those events at their Eagle Landing golf course leading up to the 1990 general election.

In the 1990 Post and Courier article following the election, Democrat Party spokesperson, Sandra Kite, was quoted as saying "They were well-financed and able to put out political propaganda that we couldn't combat. The Republicans could have run Saddam Hussein and won the election." She failed to say the Republicans had the best qualified candidates.

Before deciding whether to put the party resources behind these candidates, each one was vetted for qualifications and integrity, according to Chairman Copeland.

In the case of Jim Rozier, the candidate for Supervisor who was an executive with Playtex Corporation, upon learning that he wanted to return to his native Berkely County, State Representative Henry Brown invited him to a Republican Party fundraiser, a donkey softball game at Hanahan High School baseball field. There, Brown and Copeland met with him about running for Supervisor on the Republican ticket. He was ready.

Shortly after the meeting in Hanahan, Rozier and his wife Kathy were invited by Governor Carroll Campbell to the National Republican Governors Conference in Hilton Head. At that event, Chairman Copeland said to Mr. Rozier that the party only wanted candidates who were willing to work hard for their own elections. Before Rozier could respond, his wife said to Copeland, "Obviously you don't know Jim Rozier. He works very hard at everything he does." Once Rozier announced, he put himself into campaign mode, knocking on hundreds of doors throughout the county and mailing out hundreds of brochures outlining his qualifications and goals.

Page 4A-THE BERKELEY INDEPENDENT

Moncks Corner, SC, September 19, 1990

COMMENTARY

The responsibility of voting

By Jim Rozier
Candidate for Berkeley County Supervisor

The citizens of Berkeley County have an opportunity this November 6th we have never had in a general election. We will have a choice of candidates for almost every office.

With this opportunity comes responsibility. The responsibility is to select the most qualified candidate to carry out the duties of each office. This could be the most important decision we, as voters, will make for our county in the next decade. Why? We will be choosing the people who will lead Berkeley County into the 21st century.

The candidates elected will shape the future of Berkeley County. This future is too important to put in the hands of unqualified people. With this in mind it becomes even more important to VOTE and to VOTE for the most qualified candidate.

Learn as much as you can about each candidate. Attend forums when possible, ask questions that determine qualifications, call each candidate and ask any questions not answered to your satisfaction. Remember, you are the tax payer and you have a right to know.

All anyone can ask of you is you learn as much as you can about each candidate, make your decision based on qualifications, and then VOTE your convictions. A VOTE cast should not be considered against any candidate, but rather for the future of Berkeley County.

Please vote on November 6th.

94

On election day, after the votes were counted, Rozier had garnered 53.8 percent of the votes cast in that race.

The sheriff's race was not much different. Candidate Ray Isgett campaigned very hard, also knocking on hundreds of doors. When the votes were counted Isgett collected 55% of votes cast in that race.

Pictured following taking office in 1991, Jim Rozier, Wade Arnette, and Ray Isgett, with County Councilman Bob Call

Berkeley changes political landscape

By ARLIE PORTER
Of the Post-Courier staff

●Editorial; more on Election '90
... 3-A, 10-A, 1-B — 5-B

Berkeley County Republicans out-spent, out-advertised and out-publicized their Democratic opponents.

Tuesday, they cashed in.

And Wednesday, Republican Ray Isgett, who defeated two-term incumbent sheriff M.C. Cannon by what was considered a stunning margin, was already looking at how to put the sheriff's department in order.

"Preacher and Wrenn are out as far as I'm concerned," Isgett said of top deputy Jim Preacher and chief narcotics officer Sidney Wrenn, loyal followers of Cannon.

"I just don't believe that I can work with them effectively," Isgett said, adding that if the officers haven't resigned by Jan. 1 when he takes office, he'll fire them.

Isgett said he will hire Jim

Meade, a former part-time St. Stephen police officer and Isle of Palms police chief, who recently criticized the sheriff's department for its handling of the investigation into two drug-related murders in St. Stephen.

Meanwhile, Isgett said he was amazed that he defeated Cannon by the number of votes he did. He received 13,367 votes, or 59.6 percent, to Cannon's 9,035 votes, or 40.3 percent of the votes, according to unofficial results.

"It's a mandate," Isgett said. "Everybody was in the mood for change. A lot of things have happened in the last year, and people recognized the lack of professionalism in the department. They said, 'We do have a voice and we're going to show it.'"

Please see BERKELEY, Page 12-A

from Page 1-A

About 70 percent of registered voters voted, a fantastic turnout, election commission officer John Trout said.

"The turnout was high because it's the first time in the history of Berkeley County that there's been a full slate of candidates on both sides," Trout said, adding that many voters also came out to oppose the local option sales tax.

Overall, Republicans captured five of nine contested races.

An ecstatic Earl Copeland, chairman of the county Republican Party, said the results "were beyond our wildest dreams."

He attributed the party's victories to having sound, professional candidates on the ticket.

Democrats were shocked by the results of the sheriff's and supervisor's race, said party spokesman Sandra Kite, who attributed the GOP victories to dirty campaigning.

Cannon and county probate judge William W. "Pee Wee" Peagler, who was running for supervisor, have between them more than a half-century of public service in Berkeley County.

Republican businessman Jim Rozier defeated Peagler by a margin of 11,859 votes, or 53.8 percent, to 10,139.

Peagler attributed his loss to Rozier spending more money on advertising, including two television

ads, and "his insinuation that I would raise taxes, which I didn't say."

"I think it was a mortal blow," Mrs. Kite said of Rozier's tactic.

The same kind of campaigning held true for the sheriff's race, and also hurt Cannon, Mrs. Kite said.

"They were well-financed and were able to put out political propaganda that we couldn't combat," Mrs. Kite said. "The Republicans could have put up Saddam Hussein and won the election by taking the same tactics they used against the sheriff."

In response to Mrs. Kite's charges, Copeland agreed that Cannon and Peagler were hurt by negative publicity, "but it was all true."

Clerk of Court Mary Brown was the the only winning Democratic candidate on hand Tuesday night at the spacious Democrat headquarters in Goose Creek, where a celebration party of hundreds of Democrats was to have taken place.

While the Democrats "are down, but not out," they'll rise out of the ashes like the legendary phoenix, Mrs. Kite said.

Republicans, meanwhile, celebrated the fact that council member Lottie Altman is another type bird — lame duck — and hailed the election results as proof of the advent of a two-party system, something unheard of in traditionally Democrat Berkeley County until Republicans

hit the scene two years ago.

Republican coroner's candidate Wade Arnette soundly defeated Democrat Milton Scott by 13,030 votes to 8,919, and Republican Steve Vaughn defeated Mrs. Altman for the County Council District 5 seat. Vaughn received 2,390 votes to Mrs. Altman's 1,380.

Republicans now hold a 5-4 majority on County Council.

The GOP also will take over the register of mesne conveyence office after Cynthia Forte defeated Democrat Mildred Hood. Mrs. Forte, who is now deputy RMC, received 12,673 votes, Mrs. Hood 8,935.

Democrat Mary Brown won her third term for clerk of court, defeating Republican Joan Moore by 15,207 votes to 6,639, and Democrat Nancy Whaley, currently deputy probate judge, won the probate judge seat by defeating Republican challenger William Hutto by 11,950 votes to 9,699.

In County Council District 8, Democrat council member Bernice Friendly defeated Republican Marvin Mitchum, 1,676-1,483. And in District 4, Democrat James Dangerfield survived a Republican challenge from Robert Glover by 1,002-944.

Democrat council members Julius Barnes and F. Marion Peagler ran unopposed.

Following the 1990 election, Berkeley County saw the greatest change in 100 years. The new Supervisor and Sheriff wasted no time in reorganizing the two largest departments in Berkeley County government.

The new Berkeley County Coroner, Wade Arnette and the new RMC, office of public land records, Cindy Forte immediately began the improvements on which they had campaigned.

By 2002, every Berkeley county-wide constitutional office was held by people who filed as Republicans.

The Republican Party knew it had the attention of the voters and the media when this and other cartoons were published by John Vernelson in the Goose Creek Gazette.

★ ★

CHAPTER 14

James H. Rozier, Jr., A Born Leader

★ ★

Supervisor James H. Rozier, Jr.

Supervisor Rozier not only held the position of the county's chief executive, he was also chairman of Berkeley County Council. He now had a working majority on Berkeley County Council, who held the same governing philosophy as he. Right off, he put together a professional administrative team of department heads who would carry out the mandate for change that was given him by the voters.

He set about to become a member of numerous Lowcountry organizations so that Berkeley County would have a greater voice and influence in matters affecting the citizens of Berkeley and the Lowcountry region. He became Chairman of the Charleston Naval Complex Redevelopment Authority following the closing of Charleston Naval Shipyard.

[19]"His family was the most important part of his life. He enjoyed announcing the Berkeley Stags High School football games, attending Clemson football games, traveling, fishing, and talking. He was passionate about Mepkin Abbey and conserving Berkeley County. Jim was well known for his friendliness, generosity, sense of humor, memorable storytelling, diplomatic nature, charisma and positivity."

"Jim was born October 2, 1941, in Charleston, SC, the oldest of two children of the late James Hewlette Rozier, Sr. and Agnes Virginia Jaudon. He was a graduate of Berkeley High School and studied at Clemson University. He served as Berkeley County Supervisor for 16 years from 1990 – 2006. As Supervisor, he was the Chief Executive Officer for all County government operations and served as Chairman of County Council. While supervisor he led the County through an era of significant economic growth, attracting more than eight and one

---

19 James H Rozier Obituary: J. Henry Stuhr Inc., Northwoods Chapel

half billion dollars of industrial investment, creating more than 43,000 total jobs. Prior to becoming the Berkeley County Supervisor, he spent 30 years in national and international corporate management and operating of his own small businesses; these included Whispering Pines Memorial Gardens and Pet Rest Cemetery and Cremation Services, for which he was awarded the Small Businessman of the Year award in 1988 by the Berkeley County Chamber of Commerce. He also served as the Berkeley County Accommodations Tax Advisory Committee Chairman. He was instrumental in helping Mepkin Abbey develop their columbarium. Most recently he was a business consultant with his company The Rozier Group, LLC.

He served on the following Boards and Commissions: Board of Trustees for Trident Medical Center, Board of Directors of both the Berkeley County and Charleston Metro Chambers of Commerce, Board of Directors of the South Carolina Association of Counties, President of the State Administrators and Supervisors Association, President of the State County Council Coalition, Chairman of Berkeley, Charleston, Dorchester Regional Transportation Authority, Past President of the State Regional Council of Governments, Chairman of the Governor's Rural Summit, Clemson University Board of Visitors, National Commission on Globalization of all U.S. Counties, the BEST Committee, Chairman of the BEST Personnel and Finance Committee, Second Vice President, First Vice President and President of the South Carolina Association of Counties, Chairman of the BCD Council of Governments and Vice Chair of the National Association of Counties' Community and Economic Development Steering Committee, Farmers & Merchants Bank Board of Directors,

Clemson University's Board of Advisors for Public Service and Agriculture, the Board of Directors of the South Carolina Aquarium, the Charleston Southern University Board of Visitors, the Advisory Board for the Jim Self Center on the Future of Clemson University and SCDOT 1st Congressional District Highway Commissioner 2012 – 2016. He was elected Chairman of SCDOT in 2015. He was a member and President of Lord Berkeley Conservation Trust. He was active in Moncks Corner United Methodist Church, serving on numerous committees. He also served many roles within his community and various charitable organizations."

[20]"Berkeley County, SC (WCBD)- Longtime voice of the Berkeley Stags and former Berkeley County Supervisor Jim Rozier passed away on February 6, 2019.

For nearly 30 years, Jim Rozier served as the announcer at Berkeley high school football games. It was a volunteer position that was very important to him. Berkeley High School said that he rarely missed a game and so they called him the "Voice of the Stags".

The legacy left behind by Jim Rozier can be seen all around Berkeley County. Those who knew him say that he spent his entire life giving back to people. Berkeley High School says that their football program was enhanced by his presence on Friday nights where he served as the announcer for the Stags Football team since 1990. The Berkeley High School football department says that each year Jim was one of the first people to ask for the Stags football schedule. He even planned his family vacations around the games.

---

20 WCBD Channel 2 TV Tribute February 6, 2019

Steven Steele, principal at Berkeley High School, says "Friday nights were something special to him, because he got to see achievement. He used to always say he loved seeing the young people out here on Friday nights... Everyone knew Mr. Jim's voice. He made a wonderful environment for everyone in town."

"Berkeley High School says that there will not be a football game where Jim Rozier won't be thought of and missed".

Jim Rozier was also a man of faith. He treated everyone alike. He was not afraid of what others thought or said, he lived his faith. Those who attended his funeral witnessed the gospel music that he loved sung by an all African-American local church choir. That was the respect that he gave and received from citizens of Berkeley County, regardless of race or other factors.

Wednesday, September 6, 2000

Photo by Jim Polk

Berkeley County Supervisor Jim Rozier, in accordance with dictates from the U.S. Supreme Court, helped lead a spontaneous prayer from the stands at the Berkeley High game Friday.

Prayers still take place

By JIM POLK
Monitor Staff

The voice of Berkeley High football Jim Rozier has joined the movement to continue pre-game prayer in accordance with the dictates of the recent national Supreme Court decision.

No longer able to offer prayer across the public address system, Rozier moved into the home stands prior to the Stag's game with Battery Creek and led a spontaneous and voluntary prayer.

Rozier had no trouble getting Mary Ames Brown, wife of Berkeley High Coach Jerry Brown, to offer an unrehearsed prayer. Rozier also had no trouble getting the majority of the crowd to stand and face Ms. Brown in silence with heads bowed. Unable to hear the prayer, the crowd nonetheless offered silent prayers of their own and joined in a collective "Amen".

"This is actually a more visible sign of reverence before God," said Rozier. "In many ways it takes the prayer from simple ritual to a higher level of commitment."

He was also an encourager and role model to young people. He publicly called attention to the cost to society for those who make bad personal choices that can ruin, not only the life of that person, but also affects everyone around them.

When to know how to make your best choice!

Deciding not to use illegal drugs including alcohol and cigarettes when you are under 21, is important for your future. More and more businesses, people and governments are demanding you not use bad habit drugs. They are not only costly for any one person, they are costly for our entire society. They raise the cost of law enforcement and the judicial system. We are all part of the problem and we can all be a part of the solution if we work together to find better ways.

Jim Rozier
Berkeley County Supervisor

BERKELEY/DORCHESTER

JAMES H. ROZIER, JR. HIGHWAY

Staff Photo by Warren Wise

Berkeley County Supervisor Jim Rozier says he hopes to plant trees or flowering shrubs in the median of U.S. Highway 52 between Goose Creek and Moncks Corner. That stretch of road bears his name.

As Supervisor, Rozier was a tenacious advocate for Berkeley County. When Charleston County government attempted to annex Daniel Island after the City of Charleston annexed it into the city, he forcefully and clearly made the case to the island residents in a meeting on Daniel Island as to why they should stay a part of Berkeley County. He made the case on several levels. He also took the Berkeley Superintendent of Education with him to the meeting. In one newspaper account the writer said that Jim Rozier was a "hell of a fighter."

Why Daniel Island should stay

I do not normally respond to letters to the editor written about Berkeley County or me. However, there have been a couple of letters written about me in reference to the annexation of Daniel Island and our pro-business attitude that I must respond to in order to correct some incorrect information.

First, let me assure everyone that we want Daniel Island to stay in Berkeley County. We believe the citizens of Daniel Island are better served staying in Berkeley County, and our county is better for having them as part of our team.

When questioned about how important the tax base is on Daniel Island, I answered that the tax base is not significant today but will be very significant in the future. However, I also said that this is not about taxes, but is about what is best for people; all people in the region.

As to our industry-friendly attitude, we are industry friendly because industry does the following:

❑ Creates jobs. Some people have very short memories and seem to forget the fear this region felt when the Navy base closed.

❑ These jobs create individual incomes (median family incomes in Berkeley County increased by 25 percent from 1990 to 1997 and continue to grow). These new dollars spent in our region have allowed for unprecedented growth and success for small business firms.

❑ Industrial growth in South Carolina has provided the additional tax dollars that allow the Legisla-

ture to provide a state-funded reduction in our property taxes. Industries, even with the tax incentives, still pay a very large share of the total bill (fee-in-lieu-of taxes received from industry in 1990 was $660,000. When construction is finished, on those under construction, our annual collection will exceed $14 million. The share of the total property taxes paid by the homeowner in Berkeley County has decreased due to the amount now being paid by industry).

❑ There is some concern that industry causes a significant increase in student population in our public schools. This has not happened in Berkeley County. In fact, the number of students decreased while we had the greatest industrial growth years.

Our interest and support of industry stem from our desire to better serve people. It takes money to provide better services. We think it's better to have these additional dollars come from industry growth rather than from higher taxes. This direction has worked and continues to work for the citizens of Berkeley County.

If you would like information about how the additional revenue from industry has been used to provide better services and reduce property taxes, call or drop by the office. We will be happy to provide you with a report card on our accomplishments.

Working together we have had great accomplishments in the past decade. Working together and building on these accomplishments, our future is bright.

JIM ROZIER
Berkeley County Supervisor
223 N. Live Oak Drive
Moncks Corner

Rozier fought on every front that affected his constituents. He worked with Charleston and Dorchester Counties to create a rural transportation authority, Rural Transportation Management Authority (RTMA) to serve the people of the region who lived outside the metropolitan areas. Berkeley County native Will Hutto served as the first Executive Director.

Mary Beth Martin/The Independent

The Berkeley-Charleston-Dorchester Rural Transportation Management Association on Monday celebrated the start of rural transportation services to the tri-county area. William Hutto, RTMA executive director, greeted Jim Rozier as he steps off a bus.

When Jim Rozier took office in 1991, the Berkeley County credit rating on Standard and Poore, the New York based national credit rating service was "Stable", not unlike most other local governments in South Carolina. However, being the salesman that he was, he felt he could improve that rating, saving his constituents a lot of money over the long haul. He took a few other Berkeley County Officials with him to New York to meet with a representative of Standard and Poore.

A Charleston Post and Courier article by Business reporter Dan Parker on June 2, 1993 covered the trip. Jim made a presentation to S&P Director of Municipal Surveillance, Jon Reichert. As always, he had all the documented evidence well organized. Jim was quoted in the article, "Our presentation to them showed that Berkeley County is financially sound and stable. Our fund balance has grown considerably over the past two years" (1991 when he took office).

As a consequence of that meeting, S&P upgraded its rating to a "Positive" rating, one that almost no local government had obtained.

Berkeley's credit rating is looking up

By DAN PARKER
Of The Post and Courier staff

Berkeley County was the only government in the tri-county area to receive a positive outlook for having an improved bond credit rating in the future, according to a major credit rating company.

The possibility of naval base closings hurt bond rating outlooks for local governments, said Jon Reichert, director of municipal surveillance for Standard & Poor's, a New York City credit rating firm.

However, Berkeley County's strong revenue and financial flexibility prompted Standard & Poor's to upgrade the county's outlook from "stable" to "positive," Reichert said. Another reason for the upgrade, he said, is that Berkeley County is not as dependent on the naval base as other local governments.

A government can get a loan to pay for a project by issuing bonds, which are sold to investors. Bond credit ratings measure the government's financial ability to pay off the loan and, in turn, give investors a return on their money.

A lower credit rating means governments wanting to raise money through bond sales might have to pay off the loans at higher interest rates, with the additional cost borne by taxpayers.

Eight local governments received "negative" outlooks from Standard & Poor's. They are the cities of Charleston, North Charleston, Mount Pleasant and Hanahan; Charleston County; Charleston County Park and Recreation District; Charleston County Airport District; and Dorchester County School District No. 2.

Two governments — Dorchester County and Isle of Palms — got stable outlooks.

Berkeley County Supervisor Jim

> 'Our presentation to them showed that Berkeley County is financially sound and stable. Our fund balance has grown considerably over the last two years.'
>
> Jim Rozier
> Berkeley supervisor

Rozier said industrial development helped his county get a positive outlook.

In the past two years, Berkeley County has had $499 million in industrial investment — including the expansion of the Miles plant in Bushy Park, Rozier said.

Rozier, County Council Finance Committee Chairman Eddie Dangerfield, County Finance Director

Betty Fondren and County Attorney A.J. Tothacer recently traveled to New York and made a presentation to Standard & Poor's.

"Our presentation to them showed that Berkeley County is financially sound and stable," Rozier said. "Our fund balance has grown considerably over the last two years."

The Berkeley County officials made the trip because they were preparing to issue bonds to finance the building of a new jail, a new health department and several other ventures. The county is to pay off the bonds at a relatively low interest rate of 5.429 percent.

Standard & Poor's evaluated Berkeley County at the county's request, Reichert said.

Standard & Poor's set out on its own to evaluate the rest of the local governments' financial outlooks because of the potential base closures, Reichert said.

CHAPTER 15

Ray Isgett,
A New Sheriff in Town

★ ★

Sheriff Ray Isgett with his two sons, Buddy and Danny, both deputies with
the Charleston County Sheriff's Department

Ray Isgett had quite a story of his early days as a police officer for the City of Sumter, SC, and he had a newspaper clipping from the Sumter Daily Item that verified the story.

He and other officers were answering a call about a possible kidnapping of two children. Upon entering the building, Isgett was shot in the head by the suspect. Miraculously, he survived the shooting and for the rest of his life, he wore the bullet taken out of his head by a doctor at Toumey Hospital, on a chain around his neck.

Sumter Policeman Shot In Head

City Police Sgt. Raymond O. Isgett, 35, is reportedly in satisfactory condition in The Tuomey Hospital where he is being treated for a bullet wound in the head which was inflicted when he and other police officers answered a disturbance call on Harris Street shortly after 8 p.m. Thursday.

A 25-year-old Sumter man identified as Wardell Brown of 2 Harris St. was arrested by city police, Sumter County sheriff's deputies and highway patrolmen within minutes after the shooting.

According to police reports, Brown was shot in the left side and in a foot during the attempt to apprehend him when he fled the scene. He is reported to be in satisfactory condition.

Police reports state Brown is charged with assault and battery with intent to kill. No bond has yet been set. He is under guard at the hospital by sheriff's deputies.

IN EXPLAINING the circumstances of the incident, City Police Chief L. W. Griffin said Sgt. Isgett was shot at close range with a revolver when he went to the door of the house to investigate a report that a man was holding two small children in the house at gunpoint.

The bullet reportedly struck Isgett in the left side of his forehead and exited approximately one inch from the point of entry.

Isgett reportedly fired his pistol into the house in the direction of the gunshot six times after he was hit.

Investigation of the shooting incident has been turned over to Sumter County sheriff's deputies, which is standard procedure in cases involving city law enforcement officers, according to Chief Griffin.

According to sheriff's deputies, Brown had earlier Thursday evening been involved in a disturbance at 31 Friendship Apartments.

City police were notified of the incident at the apartments and upon investigatiin at the scene of the disturbance, police learned that Brown had two small boys, Gilbert Prince, 11 and Liston Prince, 8, at 2 Harris St. with him.

THE TWO BOYS reportedly live at 2 Harris St. with their mother, Janet Prince. Brown reportedly stays at the house from time to time according to information given to deputies in the investigation.

Wher. Isgett and three other policemen arrived at the above address, the house was reportedly dark.

Isgett went to the house and the door was answered by Gilbert Prince. When Sgt. Isgett

Continued on Page 18

Sgt. Ray Isgett

Shot In Head

Ray and his wife Carol had three children who were also in law enforcement, and a brother who was a police officer for the City of Hanahan for many years.

This excerpt taken from his Charleston Post and Courier obituary upon his death in 1996 best summarizes Sheriff Isgett's outstanding career in law enforcement.

"He was an officer who distinguished himself many times in the line of duty. Known for his appreciation for pomp and ceremony, Isgett often wore a dress uniform bedecked with medals and general's stars. A well-known photograph of Isgett shows him leaning down from the saddle of a horse in a parade to speak to a girl. That picture hung in the main hallway of the sheriff's office during his tenure, and now holds a prominent place in his Summerville home.

In keeping with his style, Isgett wore on a chain around his neck the .38-caliber slug that grazed his temple during a 1974 attempt on his life while he was a drug investigator with the Sumter Police Department. Isgett served there for 10 years and was remembered fondly by his former chief, Les Griffin. "Ray was an outstanding police officer in Sumter and also in Berkeley County, and law enforcement will certainly miss his expertise," Griffin said. Isgett took risks more than once during his career. He once went unarmed into a trailer where a suspect had barricaded himself during a standoff with police. At the time, Isgett was recovering from surgery but persuaded the man to surrender peacefully.

Isgett later said he had called upon a higher power – the faith in his three black belts in martial arts.

After the attempt on his life, Isgett left narcotics work and the Sumter Police Department for crime prevention at the state level. In

1979, Governor James B. Edwards asked Isgett to form the first statewide crime prevention program. The program was a model for subsequent crime prevention efforts and became the hallmark of Isgett's career."

In 1982, he went to the SCANA Corp. as a security consultant and remained there for eight years. In 1990, Isgett won the sheriff's race in Berkeley County and served for four years before losing his re- election bid to Sheriff Wayne DeWitt. "Since the election, we've spoken many times and become good friends. I found him to be a person who truly had Berkeley County's interests at heart," DeWitt said. Isgett earned an associate's degree in criminal justice from Palmer College and a bachelor's degree from the University of South Carolina. He received postgraduate degrees from Florida State and the University of Louisville. His awards included being named 1974 Sumter Police Officer of the Year and the American Legion Bravery Award."

Ray Isgett was a big believer in both Crime Prevention Programs and proper training of all law enforcement personnel. Early in his career he became a staunch advocate for both.

In 1979, during his service as a Sumter police officer Ray was mainly responsible for the creation of a City of Sumter community crime prevention program and served as Vice Commander of the Regional Crime Prevention Unit of Sumter, Lee and Kershaw Counties. He was also president of the Crime Prevention Committee of the S. C. Law Enforcement Association. In 1978-79 Governor Jim Edwards noticed his work in the field of crime prevention and appointed him to a new position as the state's Crime Prevention Specialist.

PAGE 8A THE DAILY ITEM — SUMTER, S.C. SATURDAY, JANUARY 6, 1979

Isgett Named To State Crime Prevention Post

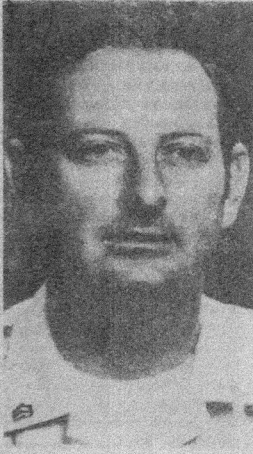

Lt. Ray Isgett, vice commander of the Regional Crime Prevention Unit for Sumter, Lee and Kershaw Counties, has been appointed state crime prevention specialist.

Gov. James B. Edwards announced Isgett's appointment to the newly-created position Friday. Isgett, 39, is president of the State Association of Crime Prevention Committee of the S.C. Law Enforcement Officer's Association.

As state crime prevention specialist, he will coordinate a statewide crime prevention program.

He will work with the state asspociation to develop such projects as a state crime prevention media campaign in conjunction with the S.C. Educational Television Network, the adoption of voluntary building security codes, development of homeowner insurance discounts for those in compliance with security codes, and to provide increased crime prevention efforts in all state law enforcement agencies.

Currently there are 22 crime prevention units in the state.

Isggett has been a member of the Sumter Police Department for 11 years, having served as a patrolman, detective, uniformed sergeant, public relations officer and supervisor.

In making the announcement, Gov. Edwards said, "It is my hope that, through the efforts of our new crime prevention specialist, all the citizens of South Caarolina will become more aware of how they can help to prevent crime."

Isgett

After being elected as Berkeley County Sheriff in 1990, Isgett embarked on a mission to turn the BCSO into one of the best trained and most disciplined Sheriff Departments in South Carolina. Previously, BCSO deputies had a reputation of being unkempt with dirty vehicles. He firmly believed that well-trained and disciplined officers started with their personal appearance and clean and well-maintained police cars. He insisted that each deputy keep his assigned vehicle clean at all times.

Sheriff Isgett was an innovator. [21]He initiated a special course taught by the Berkeley County School District to help deputies write complex crime reports that would stand up in court. The training course was recommended as a model for training at the South Carolina Criminal Justice Academy.

Hanahan News reporter Deborah Reid did an in-depth article on Sheriff Ray Isgett: The Man Behind the Change, as told by Todd Avant, on a ride-along with the sheriff, just months after he was elected.

---

21 Appendix H – Berkeley Independent: Special Course in Writing

page ten-A-THE HANAHAN NEWS-Wednesday, August 28, 1991

Ray Isgett: The man behind tl

Riding with the High Sheriff

by Deborah Reid
as told by Todd Avant

"There has been a change in Berkeley County in the past eight months," says Sheriff Ray Isgett. "I believe that people have a lot more confidence in us. We're having good success in solving crime."

Isgett, the man behind much of this change, was born in Effingham, S.C. July 9, 1939. He has been in Berkeley County for seven years.

"I enjoy being sheriff. . .This is my hobby; this is my life; this is my job; this is my occupation, my vocation, all tied up in one. Where other people go fishing, hunting, play golf, I come out, get in a police car and a uniform and ride around because I enjoy it."

His first love has always been law enforcement. "I've been in law enforcement these past 25 years in one way or another. I am very amiable to supporting in a volunteer role any law enforcement agency (where I lived)." Isgett offered his services to the past sheriff's administration but wasn't called upon. While being an administrator and in law enforcement, he saw things he thought could be done better. As a consultant to AARP, he had done ex-

ministration, I can choose the things I want to do. This is my hobby; this is my life; this is my job; this is my occupation, my vocation, all tied up in one. Where other people go fishing, hunting, play golf, I come out, get in a police car and a uniform and ride around because I enjoy it."

Voltaire

A quote he lives by comes from Voltaire, "Let us never, ever be found guilty of the good things we did not do."

"That's my motto," said Isgett.

"La Passe"

--Pass It On

Another tennant Isgett lives by is "la passe, a French term meaning "pass it on." Years ago when he was in the Air Force, stationed in California, Isgett met a man named Sterling Jones and his wife, Alice. "He sort of "took me in, almost like an adopted son. I spent much time at their house." The Joneses were in a financial position to do whatever they wanted. Isgett did not have those means, but the couple provided them, as well as moral support and encouragement. When Isgett left California, he went to Jones wanting to do something to show his gratitude for the family's kindness. He couldn't monetarily repay him, but he wouldn't be satisfied until he could compensate him "in thought".

Jones merely said, "la passe, pass it on."

Jones explained that when he was in World War II in Occupied France, he was separated from the Allies. A French underground couple took him in, fed, clothed and hid him until he could be-

Sheriff Ray Isgett

ton County. He has a brother in the Hanahan Police Department. They're a close family. "If something happens to one, it happens to all."

On patrol

On patrol Isgett pays attention to the radio for what's going on all over the county to see if a deputy has a trouble spot, needs help or advice, and monitors activities. "When I patrol, when you've done it as long as I have, it becomes second nature. If something happens out of the peripheral vision of your eye, you catch it. It may be half a block before it hits you, but you turn around, you catch on to it. The longer you're in law enforcement, the more subconsciously these things are embedded that you don't even realize (it) until it happens."

"Death on Drugs"

"I'm death on drugs, zero

116

★ ★

CHAPTER 16

Rounding Out the Winning Team

★ ★

Besides the Supervisor and Sheriffs Offices, the other two county-wide offices that were won by Republicans in 1990, and which gave Republicans the status of majority party, were the Coroner and the Register of Deeds. Both offices had always been held by Democrats.

The offices of Treasurer, Clerk of Court and Probate Judge, would also be filled by Republican candidates in succeeding elections.

Wade Arnette - Coroner

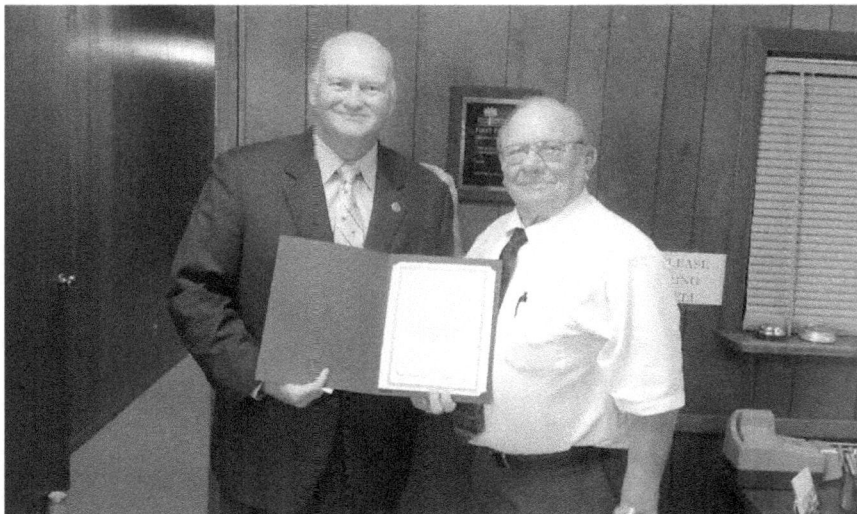

Medical Disciplinary Commission of the State Board of Medical Examiners presented by Secretary of State Mark Hammond

Wade C. Arnette was born in Dillon County, S.C. in 1932. He is a graduate of Lakeview High School in Dillon and Wingate College in North Carolina. He is a United States Air Force veteran of the Korean War discharged as a Staff Sergeant and served as Assistant Veterans Service Officer in Dillon County.

Prior to being elected as Berkeley County's first Republican coroner in 1990, Wade owned an Insurance Adjusting company. He served as Director of Statistical Research for South Carolina Department of Insurance. He also was a member of Property Loss, Research and Defense Research Institute. He later served as President of South Carolina Association of County-wide Elected Executives.

Over his more than 50 years of public service, Wade served on numerous Boards and Commissions, as well as having received numerous service awards, including South Carolina's highest civilian award, Order of Palmetto, which was presented to him on behalf to the Governor by Representative Henry E. Brown, Jr.

He served three terms, retiring in December 2002.

Wade was all about service. While running for the office of coroner, he made a campaign promise that he would hold periodic meetings with any group having dealings with the Coroner's office to find ways to make it easier for people facing the end of life, and their families. In 1991 after assuming the office, he kept that promise when he held such a meeting that was attended by representatives of police, EMS, fire and rescue personnel, funeral home directors and Hospice staff to work on such a plan.

By allowing Hospice nurses to notify his office directly of a Hospice patient's death, rather than having EMS respond with sirens and flashing lights, the family will experience a calmer and more dignified death of their loved one`.

EMS Working With Hospice For Patients

By DAVID W. MacDOUGALL
Of the Post-Courier staff

After Hospice of Charleston works six months to help a terminally ill person's family members prepare for a peaceful death at home, the flashing lights and sirens of an EMS wagon can shatter that peace, said Hospice executive director Cynthia Simpson-Byrne.

But since Berkeley County Coroner Wade Arnette took office Jan. 1, he has allowed Hospice nurses to notify his office directly so EMS is not called to the home, Ms. Simpson-Byrne said.

"He's willing to help us provide a more dignified death for the patient and the family," the hospice director said.

Ms. Simpson-Byrne spoke Wednesday at a meeting called by Arnette and attended by representatives from police, EMS, fire and rescue personnel as well as funeral home directors and Hospice staff.

"These meetings were a campaign promise," Arnette said. "We will get together with everyone who has dealings with the office on a quarterly basis."

Arnette told the group his office had handled 58 deaths since Jan. 1. "And we have responded to every part of this very large county within 45 minutes," he said.

Arnette told the group he intends to develop a multi-fatality disaster plan.

"We have Amtrak trains coming through the county. We have planes flying over us. We could have a disaster that would kill many people. I pray to God it doesn't happen but I want to be prepared if it does," Arnette said.

After Hanahan police Lt. T. Walker suggested that the coroner's office conduct seminars to help police, firefighters and paramedics deal with the grief of victims' relatives.

Arnette said he would schedule such a seminar for his next quarterly meeting.

On July 20, 2024, many friends and former colleagues of former Berkeley County Coroner Wade Arnette gathered to celebrate Wade's 92nd birthday, and for the dedication of the street, WADE ARNETT ROAD, named in his honor by the South Carolina Department of Transportation. Pictured here are: Seated, the Honoree, Wade Arnette, and former Congressman Henry E. Brown, Jr., who emceed the event. Standing, L to R, Jerry Baxley, Berkeley County Veterans Service Officer; South Carolina Secretary of State Mark Hammond; State Representative (District 99) Mark Smith; Berkeley County Coroner, Darnell Hartwell; Former Berkeley County Republican Chairman, Earl Copeland; State Representative (District 102) Joe Jefferson; Former State Representative (District 92), Joe Daning. Missing, but also there, Berkeley County Treasurer, Carolyn Umphlett, Berkeley

County Register of Deeds, Cynthia Forte, and former Berkeley County Veterans Service Officer, Clarence "Mac" McGee.

Former Berkeley County Coroner Wade Arnette, with the newly designated highway sign named in his honor.

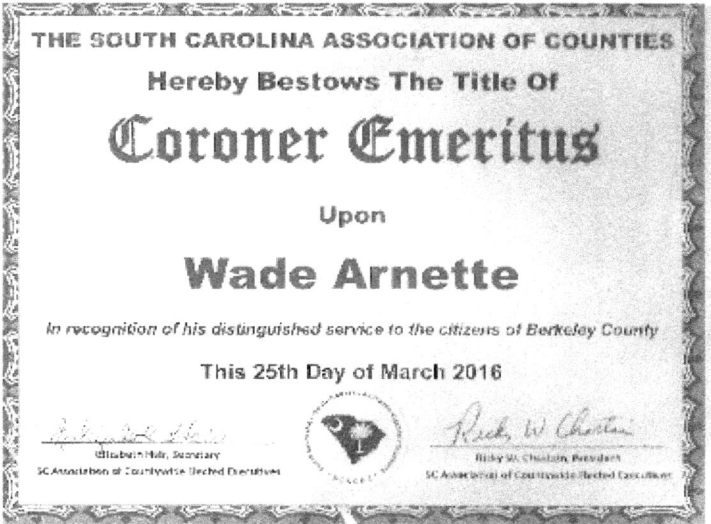

Cynthia Forte – RMC/Register of Deeds

After serving as Deputy RMC in the Berkeley County Register Mesne Conveyance Office since 1979, Cindy Forte made the decision to run for Berkeley County RMC as a Republican candidate upon the retirement of the previous Register in 1990. After winning the Republican Primary, she became a valued member of an impressive Republican Team, that adopted the campaign slogan of "From the Courthouse to the Statehouse". Cindy went on to easily win in the General Election as well. In 1997, the SC Legislature passed a bill changing the name of the office from the "Register Mesne Conveyance", which almost no one could pronounce, to the "Register of Deeds".

When she began working in the RMC office in 1979, all records in the office were recorded manually using handwritten index cards and photocopied documents. Computers were not being used at all. Upon being elected in November 1990 she had set a goal to modernize the office using the latest technology. Early in her tenure, she received funding to begin microfilming and having documents printed in small usable books. Berkeley County land records began back in 1884, and the records were kept in very large handwritten books.

Today, under her leadership, the Register of Deeds Office has a state-of-the-art computer program which is fully digitized, from cashiering to the end of the recording process. Additionally, all document images are now online for public use for the years 1974 to present, providing attorneys, title abstractors, and the general public free access to Berkeley County land records.

Cindy is now serving in her ninth term as Register of Deeds.

★ ★

CHAPTER 17

All About Teamwork/ Together We Can

★ ★

Probably the number one reason for the tremendous success in Berkeley County Government for the past thirty years has been the attitude among elected Republican officials in local, state and federal levels is that of unity of purpose. From the earliest days when Republicans became the majority party in 1990, they adopted the position of working together for the betterment of Berkeley County's citizens.

Nothing demonstrates that philosophy better than this side-by-side ads by Henry Brown and Jim Rozier.

It's all about
Team Work!

And that is true in
every business and
every profession,
including elected officials.
That has always been
my focus and objective.
There is no greater honor than serving
your fellow citizens. I am privileged to
have done that, and I look forward to
continuing to do that.

Henry E. Brown Jr.
Republican Candidate
First Congressional District
Paid Political Advertising

"Together we can!"
is still my motto,
as it was the first time
I sought to serve you.

That is the way we have built
and maintained one of the best
County Councils
in South Carolina.
And that's what we will
continue to do...
together!

Jim Rozier
Supervisor, Berkeley County

H. Allen Morris/The Independent

**Berkeley County Supervisor Jim Rozier presents
Hanahan Rep. Henry Brown Jr. a framed resolution
commending Brown with the assistance and leadership Brown displayed to help Berkeley County
receive a state grant for the BCW&SA to run water
lines to Bushy Park.**

Working together, Berkeley County Council, led by Supervisor Jim Rozier, and State Representative Henry Brown as Chairman of South Carolina House Ways and Means Committee, were successful in bringing water lines to the households of rural areas of Berkeley as well as to expand industry, which brought more and higher paying jobs to Berkeley. Working closely with South Carolina Secretary of Commerce, Robert Royall in the cabinet of Governor David Beasley, they zealously sought out and recruited new high-quality industry for Berkeley County.

Because of the political leadership of state and local government, Berkeley County became known around the world as industry and business friendly, which made recruiting new industry much easier. As a result, Berkeley became a leader of industry in South Carolina, and still today, maintains that leadership and reputation.

[22]In the 1996 Post and Courier Business section article by Chris Sosnowski, "Berkeley Industry-seekers hit triple" State Commerce Secretary Robert Royall emphasized the importance of bringing industries like Nucor Steel that will be magnets for other industries in what he referred to as "clusters". MG Industries area manager Al Bentz said that his company located in Berkeley County because Nucor being in Berkeley was the "best of several potential spots considered world-wide, and adding to that is the fact that Berkeley County is a draw for other businesses."

---

22 Appendix J - Post and Courier Business section article "Berkeley industry-seekers hit triple"

Team playing has caused Berkeley County to attract over $1 billion in new industry

No other county in the history of South Carolina has been able to attract over $1 billion in new industrial investment within less than a calendar year.

Berkeley County would have never been able to attract over $1 billion in new industrial investment within seven and one-half months of 1995, and to continue to attract new industry, if not for a concerted team effort between all three chambers of commerce in the tri-county area, the Charleston Area Alliance for Economic Development, the Governor's Office, the State Department of Commerce, Berkeley County Council and the Berkeley County School District working with one clear focus.

Those of you playing on football teams this year should do the same as we have in the tri-county area to increase economic development. By using the total-team concept with a clear focus, each of your high school teams should have one of the best years ever.

Remember, "Together, we did", and together, you can.

James Rozier
Berkeley County
Supervisor

Nucor announcement adds $50 million more

By H. Allen Morris
Independent Editor

Nucor officials cited the partnership between Berkeley County Supervisor Jim Rozier, Berkeley County Council, The Charleston Regional Trident Development Alliance, Governor David Beasley, S. C. Department of Commerce Executive Director Robert Royall and the efficiency of the employees at the Berkeley plant in deciding to add a $50 million expansion at the newly opened plant.

Nucor, the second largest steel producer in the nation, entered the Charleston region in 1995, when company officials announced a $500 million capital investment and the creation of 500 jobs averaging about $50,000 annually. This addition will create 50 more new jobs.

The expansion will add a galvanizing line, which will process approximately 400,000 tons of the company's cold-rolled sheet metal. The plant's annual production capacity of cold-rolled and hot-rolled sheets is currently 1.8 million tons.

Charles Way, President-elect of the Charleston Trident Regional Alliance served as master-of-ceremonies for the announcement at a lectern on a podium in the office building parking lot. The one-story office complex with three buildings is faced with gray stone and hunter green trim in a double line around the tops of the office complex. Looming over the offices are the tall manufacturing buildings. Nucor spends approximately $1.8 million per month to Santee Cooper for electricity they use in producing rolled cold steel.

"Since entering this market, we at Nucor have found boundless opportunities for growth and expansion," noted John D. Correnti, Nucor Vice Chairman, President and CEO. "The availability of well-trained workers, the presence of a world-renowned port, and the support we have received from the business community have provided Nucor with an extraordinary quick start time in this market, and allowed us to expand in a very short period of time."

Correnti recalled, "Two and one-half years ago on a Wednesday morning I read in *The Charlotte Observer* that Governor David Beasely had become governor of South Carolina.

"The next Saturday morning Governor Beasley and Bob Royall were in my office in Charlotte. They wanted to know what they could do to make it possible for us to locate our new plant in South Carolina.

"This is a great state in which to do business. Nucor has over $800 million in assets in South Carolina. We have plants in Florence, Darlington, Lancaster, and Swansee. We have found fair taxes, reasonable utilities and dedicated hard-working work force."

"Supervisor Jim Rozier and S. C. Secretary of Revenue Bernie Maybank also helped bring this $540 million plant and this additional $50 million plant to Berkeley County.

"We already have employed in this plant 400 people. Satellite industries serving this plant have added and will add up to 1,300 more jobs.

"Nucor has plants on 23 sites in eight states, and we chose Berkeley for this expansion.

"You can't beat this area between the excellent golfing and excellent fishing it offers.'"

"Nucor's decision to add the galvanizing line here in Berkeley County instead of its other mill locations is significant for many reasons," noted T. Graham Edwards, Chairman of The Alliance, President and CEO of Santee Cooper and founder and president of the Berkeley Highs School Academic Booster Club. "We were confident when they entered this market two years ago the Charleston Region would contribute to Nucor's ongoing success. The announcement is evidence we were right, and they were right to partner with us."

The recruitment of Nucor Steel to the Charleston region in 1995 was considered a major economic coup, and one celebrated statewide.

"About two years ago Nucor announced a $540 million mini-mill in Cainhoy. And today, Nucor selected South Carolina again," said Governor David Mulhouse Beasley. "This time Nucor will add a galvanizing production line adding 50 jobs to the Lowcountry and $40 million in investment. This is a sweet day for South Carolina's economy."

"South Carolina excels in attracting quality, value-added jobs to all parts of the state,"

See NUCOR ....Page 2A

[23]In a September 2000 article by Post and Courier Neighborhood Editor Robert Behre, Jim Rozier, talked about his and County Council's opposition to the State Ports Authority's planned location of a major port facility on Daniel Island because of environmental concerns. He made the point that he offered better alternatives. He also mentioned that Nucor had "put in protection" 5000 acres of the land they had obtained.

In conjunction, State Senator Arthur Ravenel also worked in the legislature to prevent SPA from locating on Daniel Island. On a tour of the alternative site on the old navy base, on which the author was present, Senator Ravenel made the point very forcefully to the State Ports Authority Executive Director, Bernie Groseclose, that the new port facility would never be built on Daniel Island. The senator introduced legislation that passed, and required the new terminal be built on the old navy base. A new SPA Executive Director was hired a short time later. That new facility, Hugh Leatherman Terminal, opened in March 2021.

---

23 Appendix K – Post and Courier article, A Conversation with Jim Rozier 9/7/2000

★ ★

CHAPTER 18

Lasting Change

★ ★

At the writing of this book, over thirty years after the 1990 election, Berkeley Republicans continue to maintain a majority. Every county-wide elective office, along with six of the eight County Council seats, are now held by Republicans.

APPENDIX A-1

Dennis, Edward James (1844-1904) — of Charleston County, S.C.; Berkeley County, S.C. Born in Charleston District (part now in Berkeley County), S.C., March 23, 1844. Served in the Confederate Army during the Civil War; surveyor; cotton planter; lawyer; member of South Carolina state house of representatives, 1880-82, 1884-85, 1892-93 (Charleston County 1880-82, Berkeley County 1884-85, 1892-93); member of South Carolina state senate from Berkeley County, 1894-1904; defeated, 1886, 1890; died in office 1904; delegate to South Carolina state constitutional convention from Berkeley County, 1895. Member, United Confederate Veterans. Died in Macbeth, Berkeley County, S.C., May 24, 1904 (age 60 years, 62 days). Interment at Mt. Olivet Cemetery, Cross, S.C.

APPENDIX A-2

Dennis, Edward James (1877-1930) — also known as E. J. Dennis — of Berkeley County, S.C. Born in Macbeth, Berkeley County, S.C., September 23, 1877. Lawyer; member of South Carolina state house of representatives from Berkeley County, 1900-04, 1916-18; member of South Carolina state senate from Berkeley County, 1904-06, 1910-14, 1918-22, 1926-30; died in office 1930. Methodist. Tried and acquitted in 1929 for conspiracy to violate the alcohol prohibition law. Shot and mortally wounded by Webster Lee 'Sporty' Thornley, on the street in front of the post office in Moncks Corner, S.C., and died the next day in a hospital at Charleston, Charleston County, S.C., July 25, 1930 (age 52 years, 305 days). Thornley was tried and convicted of murder; Glenn D. McKnight, who allegedly hired Thornley to murder Dennis, was tried and not convicted. Interment at St. John's Baptist Churchyard, Pinopolis, S.C.

APPENDIX A-3

Dennis, Rembert Coney (1915-1992) — also known as Rembert C. Dennis — of Moncks Corner, Berkeley County, S.C. Born in Pinopolis, Berkeley County, S.C., August 27, 1915. Democrat. Lawyer; member of South Carolina state house of representatives from Berkeley County, 1938-42; member of South Carolina state senate, 1942-88 (Berkeley County 1942-66, 14th District 1966-84, 37th District 1984-88); delegate to Democratic National Convention from South Carolina, 1944, 1948 (alternate), 1952, 1956, 1960; candidate for justice of South Carolina state supreme court, 1956. Baptist. Member, American Bar Association; Sigma Alpha Epsilon; Freemasons; Scottish Rite Masons; Shriners; Lions; Woodmen of the World; Blue Key. Died June 20, 1992 (age 76 years, 298 days). Interment at St. John's Baptist Churchyard, Pinopolis, S.C.

APPENDIX B

This appendix covers only the sections of the South Carolina Home Rule Act of 1975 that are relevant to this book. The full version can be found online at the South Carolina Code of Laws, **Title 4 – Counties**.

CHAPTER 9
County Government

SECTION 4-9-20. Designation of permissible alternative forms of government.

The alternate forms of government which may be adopted pursuant to Section 4-9-10 shall be one of the following:

(a) Council form as set forth in Article 3;

(b) Council-supervisor form as set forth in Article 5;

(c) Council-administrator form as set forth in Article 7;

(d) Council-manager form as set forth in Article 9;

(e) Board of commissioners form as set forth in Article 11.

HISTORY: 1962 Code Section 14-3702; 1975 (59) 692.

For the counties of Berkeley, Colleton, Marion, Orangeburg, Marlboro and Williamsburg, the county board of commissioners form of government as prescribed in Article 11 of this chapter.

The governing body in those counties adopting the county board of commissioners form of government provided for in this article shall consist of not less than four nor more than twelve commissioners, as may be determined by the General Assembly for each county electing to adopt the form of government provided for in this article, all of whom shall be qualified electors of the county.

ARTICLE 5

Council-Supervisor Form of County Government

(Form No. 2)

SECTION 4-9-410. Membership of council; election, term, and compensation of supervisor.

The council in those counties adopting the council-supervisor form of government provided for in this article shall consist of not less than two nor more than twelve members who are qualified electors of the county. The supervisor shall serve as chairman and vote only to break tie votes. The supervisor shall be a qualified elector of the county, elected at large from the county in the general election for a term of two or four years.

The compensation for the supervisor shall be prescribed by the council by ordinance. The council shall not reduce or increase the compensation of the supervisor during the term of office for which he was elected. (Form No. 3)

SECTION 4-9-610. Membership of council; election and term of members.

The council in those counties adopting the council-administrator form of government provided for in this article shall consist of not less than three nor more than twelve members who are qualified electors of the county. Council members shall be elected in the general election for terms of two or four years commencing on the first of January next following their election.

HISTORY: 1962 Code Section 14-3740; 1975 (59) 692.

SECTION 4-9-620. Employment and qualifications of administrator; compensation; term of employment; procedure for removal.

The council shall employ an administrator who shall be the administrative head of the county government and shall be responsible for the administration of all the departments of the county government which the council has the authority to control. He shall be employed with regard to his executive and administrative qualifications only, and need not be a resident of the county at the time of his employment. The term of employment of the administrator shall be at the pleasure of the council and he shall be entitled to such compensation for his services as the council may determine. The council may, in its discretion, employ the administrator for a definite term. If the council determines to remove the county administrator, he shall be given a written statement of the reasons alleged for the proposed removal and the right to a hearing thereon at a public meeting of the council. Within five days after the notice of removal is delivered to the administrator he may file with the council a written request for a public hearing. This hearing shall be held at a council meeting not earlier than twenty days nor later than thirty days after the request is filed. The administrator may file with the council a written reply not later than five days before the hearing. The removal shall be stayed pending the decision at the public hearing.

APPENDIX C

Straight Across   *by H. Allen Morris*

You ain't seen nothing yet!

ember 9, 1988

Now that the disgracefully nasty presidential race, and our almost equally nasty Auditor's race and County Council District 3 race are all over, we can relax a bit from the overwhelming political rhetoric we have been bombarded with these past six months.

Don't fool yourself, you ain't seen nothing yet, if you think these races were a bit hot and dirty. And for those who thought the races were uninteresting and you prefer a lot of political whirligig, just wait until 1990. That's when a carnucopia of local races will be hotly contested. You can bet your sweet bippy that almost every race from the Governor, on the state level, to Berkeley County Supervisor and County Council on the local level will have opposition for incumbents.

It's no secret stellar Democrats, Lt. Gov. Nick Theodore, S. C. Attorney General Travis Medlock and S. C. Comptroller General Earl Morris, all would just dearly love to have a chance at the Governor's seat.

On the local level Berkeley County Supervisor Johnnie T. Flynn is bound to have opposition again. This time around both Judge of Probate Wm. "Pee Wee" Peagler and newly named Berkeley County Small businessman of the Year, James Rozier are being touted for that position. If Rozier decides to offer he will run as a Republican, which will be the first time a Republican has

challenged that position.

Sheriff M. C. Cannon has already stated he will run again in 1990. He will be challenged in the Democratic primary by Osborne Morris, who ran as a Republican against Cannon before Morris was named Moncks Corner Police Chief and was fired from the same job.

Several other people in law enforcement are looking at the possibility of running for Sheriff. One may announce as a Republican since some believe Sheriff Cannon is more vulnerable than ever due to receiving a preponderance of negative publicity from multiple sources. Cannon will be a formidable candidate under any circumstances since he enjoys a hard core of devoted fans who would do anything, short of breaking the law, for him.

If Judge Peagler gives up his Judge of Probate post, defeated Republican County Council District 3 member, Merrill Cox has been mentioned as a possible candidate. There will also probably be a Democratic Candidate

If Coroner William Smith decides or does not decide to offer again, the Coroner's slot is certain to have both Democratic and Republican challenges.

You can also expect Democratic challenges to County Council districts 6 and 8 and perhaps a Republican challenge to the District 6 seat held before and since Home Rule began by Francis Marion Peagler. While it is recognized

Councilman Peagler will almost be impossible to beat, if he chooses to run again, the Berkeley County Republican party is feeling its oats.

Though newly elected House of Representative member Jack Williams is more a Republican than a Democrat, he may also hold opposition since this will be his first term. Much depends on how well he adapts to and performs in his new position. On the other hand, when good man Jack finds out the detritus House of Representative members with which they have to deal, he may decide one term is enough.

Win or lose this time around, understand there is a growing two-political party system in Berkeley County now. If anyone ever doubted it before this election, Republican Chairman Earl Copeland has certainly erased all doubt. Not only is Chairman Earl a strong and focused leader of the Republican Party, he is also a self-appointed watchdog against even the hint of Democratic Party cronyism, subterfuge or anything which has even a shadow of wrong doing. Watch out, political good ole' boys, Earl Re-

publican man is not going away. He's going to continue to circle like a Hawk over Democratic Party doings watching for minuscule cracks in their wall of legendary strength.

Ain't it fun?

Next week look for my usual in-depth analysis of the Berkeley County vote, if any of you might be the slightest bit interested.

ALL ABOUT TOWN

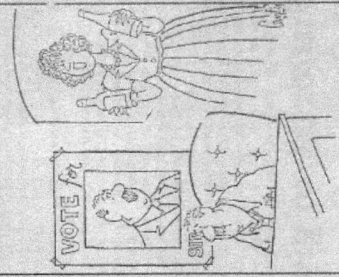

"Sid, what goes best with defeat..red or white wine?"

APPENDIX D

BC., June 13, 1990

Straight Across   by H. Allen Morris

Is a November Republican sweep possible?

Be assured Republican party chairman, hawk-eyed, vociferous voiced chairman B. Earl Copeland, wasn't kidding when he said Tuesday night he believed a Republican sweep in Berkeley County is now possible in the November 6 general election.

A 17% minority of Berkeley County residents, eligible to vote, have decided the definitive political contenders in the general election. The exception is for the Democratic party nominee for Coroner which will be decided in a run-off between Rev. Milton Scott and Deputy Coroner "Chuck" Langston.

The future political focus of Berkeley County, which will carry well into this last decade before we reach the 21st century, will be sealed in 4 months, 23 days from this date.

Not too many years ago, primary winners were considered, in this one-party county, automatic victors in November.

Know well under Chairman Copeland's strong leadership, Republican candidates will mount well organized campaigns. Know also Chairman Copeland will do all within his power to make his fondest dream come true – a Republican dominated county government.

Meek and mild Democratic Party Chairman H. L. Dukes does not cotton to wild and sometime hysterical protesta-

tions for which vociferous voice chairman Earl is well known.

Let's look at the stage for the general election in Berkeley County.

Democrats have elected the first black candidate for Governor who will run against one of the most popular Governors South Carolina has had in recent times.

If the national Democratic party smells a possible upset, such as they enjoyed in Virginia with the election of their first black governor and with the victory in New York City with their first black Mayor, then they might be tempted to throw a bundle of money into Mitchell's campaign.

Not to be outdone, Gov. Carroll Campbell Jr. also has access to national Republican party mega-bucks. If this happens, there could be an unusually high voter turn-out in the November off-year election. It is possible Berkeley County Republican candidates chances would be improved by hitching a ride on Campbell's coat-tails just as candidates enjoyed an extra push when President George Bush won.

It's entirely possible Republican candidates might do well in

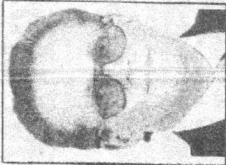

challenger Jim Meade, the knowledge he had not won by 80%, and won by 60% should cause him a bit of concern.

The concern would come when realized if Meade's vote is added to both that of Osborne Morris and Ray Isgett, the Republican nominee, the possible vote then shows Cannon losing the county-wide vote at 43% of the vote to Isgett's 57%. Both Morris and Meade said earlier they will support Isgett if he became the Republican candidate for Sheriff.

In the County County District 4 race it is also probable incumbent Eddie Dangerfield could lose Republican challenger Bob Glover did not do a massive amount of campaigning and still won easily. Also the District 4 area is becoming more Republican in its demographic composition. Add to that candidate Glover has heavily pushed his involvement in the Berkeley

Berkeley County without that extra push.

I suspect incumbent Democratic candidate for Sheriff M. C. now realizes this. While there was an initial burst of energy from Cannon family members and supporters after learning he beat

Chamber of Commerce Leadership Berkeley program and his chances improve.

A similar scenario could happen in County Council District 5 where Republican candidate Steve Vaughn will challenge incumbent Democratic candidate Lottie Altman, one of the more visionary members of County Council.

This hypothetical scenario would give us 5 Republican County Council members and 3 Democrats.

That's only a glimpse at the November possibilities.

Because all totals will not be certified until this Thursday, I will be doing my traditional analysis for the June 20 issue.

One final word for this week. Many candidate supporters, and others who declared our poll printed in the June 6 issue was way off base – from 40% to 70% wrong, might examine the actual vote totals. With a stated declaration there would a 10% plus or minor factor, we were amazingly correct. In the Supervisor's race between Flynn and Peagler our projections matched perfectly with the actual totals. Yes, it is nice to be vindicated. And yes, the declarations that we were vastly wrong, did cause me some trepidation. What is particular pleasing to me, is not we were right, it is the people who responded to our poll were right!

APPENDIX E

Berkeley changes political landscape

By ARLIE PORTER
Of the Post-Courier staff

●Editorial; more on Election '90
... 3-A, 10-A, 1-B — 5-B

Berkeley County Republicans outspent, out-advertised and out-publicized their Democratic opponents.

Tuesday, they cashed in.

And Wednesday, Republican Ray Isgett, who defeated two-term incumbent sheriff M.C. Cannon by what was considered a stunning margin, was already looking at how to put the sheriff's department in order.

"Preacher and Wrenn are out as far as I'm concerned," Isgett said of top deputy Jim Preacher and chief narcotics officer Sidney Wrenn, loyal followers of Cannon.

"I just don't believe that I can work with them effectively," Isgett said, adding that if the officers haven't resigned by Jan. 1 when he takes office, he'll fire them.

Isgett said he will hire Jim Meade, a former part-time St. Stephen police officer and Isle of Palms police chief, who recently criticized the sheriff's department for its handling of the investigation into two drug-related murders in St. Stephen.

Meanwhile, Isgett said he was amazed that he defeated Cannon by the number of votes he did. He received 13,367 votes, or 59.6 percent, to Cannon's 9,035 votes, or 40.3 percent of the votes, according to unofficial results.

"It's a mandate," Isgett said. "Everybody was in the mood for change. A lot of things have happened in the last year, and people recognized the lack of professionalism in the department. They said, 'We do have a voice and we're going to show it.'"

Please see BERKELEY, Page 12-A

---

from Page 1-A

About 70 percent of registered voters voted, a fantastic turnout, election commission officer John Trout said.

"The turnout was high because it's the first time in the history of Berkeley County that there's been a full slate of candidates on both sides," Trout said, adding that many voters also came out to oppose the local option sales tax.

Overall, Republicans captured five of nine contested races.

An ecstatic Earl Copeland, chairman of the county Republican Party, said the results "were beyond our wildest dreams."

He attributed the party's victories to having sound, professional candidates on the ticket.

Democrats were shocked by the results of the sheriff's and supervisor's race, said party spokesman Sandra Kite, who attributed the GOP victories to dirty campaigning.

Cannon and county probate judge William W. "Pee Wee" Peagler, who was running for supervisor, have between them more than a half-century of public service in Berkeley County.

Republican businessman Jim Rozier defeated Peagler by a margin of 11,859 votes, or 53.8 percent, to 10,139.

Peagler attributed his loss to Rozier spending more money on advertising, including two television ads, and "his insinuation that I would raise taxes, which I didn't say."

"I think it was a mortal blow," Mrs. Kite said of Rozier's tactic.

The same kind of campaigning held true for the sheriff's race, and also hurt Cannon, Mrs. Kite said.

"They were well-financed and were able to put out political propaganda that we couldn't combat," Mrs. Kite said. "The Republicans could have put up Saddam Hussein and won the election by taking the same tactics they used against the sheriff."

In response to Mrs. Kite's charges, Copeland agreed that Cannon and Peagler were hurt by negative publicity, "but it was all true."

Clerk of Court Mary Brown was like the only winning Democratic candidate on hand Tuesday night at the spacious Democrat headquarters in Goose Creek, where a celebration party of hundreds of Democrats was to have taken place.

While the Democrats "are down, but not out," they'll rise out of the ashes like the legendary phoenix, Mrs. Kite said.

Republicans, meanwhile, celebrated the fact that council member Lottie Altman is another type bird — lame duck — and hailed the election results as proof of the advent of a two-party system, something unheard of in traditionally Democrat Berkeley County until Republicans hit the scene two years ago.

Republican coroner's candidate Wade Arnette soundly defeated Democrat Milton Scott by 13,030 votes to 8,919, and Republican Steve Vaughn defeated Mrs. Altman for the County Council District 5 seat. Vaughn received 2,390 votes to Mrs. Altman's 1,380.

Republicans now hold a 5-4 majority on County Council.

The GOP also will take over the register of mesne conveyence office after Cynthia Forte defeated Democrat Mildred Hood. Mrs. Forte, who is now deputy RMC, received 12,673 votes, Mrs. Hood 8,935.

Democrat Mary Brown won her third term for clerk of court, defeating Republican Joan Moore by 15,207 votes to 6,639, and Democrat Nancy Whaley, currently deputy probate judge, won the probate judge seat by defeating Republican challenger William Hutto by 11,950 votes to 9,699.

In County Council District 8, Democrat council member Bernice Friendly defeated Republican Marvin Mitchum, 1,676-1,483. And in District 4, Democrat James Dangerfield survived a Republican challenge from Robert Glover by 1,002-944.

Democrat council members Julius Barnes and F. Marion Peagler ran unopposed.

APPENDIX F

November 7, 1990

STRAIGHT ACROSS

Voters speak with loud voice

by H. ALLEN MORRIS

It was an incredible election in almost every way. The weekend before, new Republican victor for Supervisor Jim Rozier and I chatted briefly about how I had observed and recorded these past 13 years, the change from one-man control of local government to the possibility of a strong two party system.

Then we had no way of knowing just how passionate voters in Berkeley County were going to be in making that possibility a reality.

I have been a witness to a political system in Berkeley County when the people who have no connections to elected officials had almost no hope of a voice in government. I have seen a system disgustingly corrupt slowly wither away because people grew increasingly wary of having their tax dollars fund special interest people and projects.

I have been a victim of that system having to bear threats to my safety and livelihood as recently as this past election. I despise intimidation and particularly attempts at revenge.

The only purpose I have ever had in what I have written about my personal political observations and beliefs is because I have believed and still believe Berkeley County residents can have a productive political system working for the good of all of its citizens and not those loyal to the incumbent power structure.

Early Tuesday morning it became obvious some major changes were in the making when information began to trickle in about the large voter turn-out all over the county.

It was a true contest between those who thought the "Good Ole' Boy" system, long a tradition in the Democratic party, should continue and those who decided with a combined loud voice to turn the "Good Ole' Boy" politicians out.

On election day we received a few calls from people who simply wanted to know who the incumbents were so they could vote against them.

The total vote displays a partnership between Berkeley County natives, new residents and a growing disenchanted black population who joined together to bring Berkeley County it's first real two party system.

They have put on notice all who may be tempted to continue traditional political favors that time is past—long past.

To those elected, they should carefully note voters have made important demands with their combined voices. They have an opportunity to put into practice their campaign promises of public accountability.

We want elected officials, when they make a mistake, are not afraid to admit it. We want elected officials to be honest with us and when they need our help to call for it. We want elected officials to give information even if it is negative.

When the public hears bad news about an elected official by that elected official first, the public has more respect for that person.

It would be foolish and naive of us to think Republicans are exempt from being "Good Ole' Boys" and once in power, might be tempted to use the system for their own benefit.

Remember "Lost Trust" legislators Robert Kahn and Rick Lee are both Republicans and what they have done to their constituents is as big an insult as politicians can make.

Republican Chairman Earl Copeland, Supervisor-elect Jim Rozier, and Sheriff-elect Ray Ispett have all been clearly told by me I have no intention of relaxing my vigilance against whatever I find in government not to be working for the people.

They both have stated publicly they are going to actively seek citizen involvement from throughout the county. That's good news.

More good news is we have enough Democrat office holders in Berkeley County to have a viable strong two-party system. Our Judge of Probate, Clerk of Court, Treasurer and four county council seats are all held by Democrats.

One the state representation level we have one Democrat senator; two Republican House members and two Democrat House members.

The total now stands at 12

Republicans and 10 Democrat local elected officials.

Now if the county Democrat Party, limping along without strong leadership, can recognamination of the vule with a clear vision their role as a valuable part, political checks and balance then we will have a strong two party system working for the people instead of against the people.

About the Independent poll

Just goes to show you scientific is not always the best way to go. However, a cursory examination of the vote resulting compared to the poll shows was 67% correct in predicting winners and in some case called the percentages almost exact. What happened in district 8, I don't know. This I know, those who won in district 8 did not win with a mandate which shows a major change in voting patterns.

The District 5 seat was decided by the enormous and the expected voter turnout in the precincts. Also from a cursory examination a significant number of those voters chose to vote a straight Republican ticket. Hence the difference.

Coming next week

We will provide a complete chart and analysis of the county wide vote next week. A quick look shows some interesting trends. Stay tuned.

143

APPENDIX G

Reprinted Article from CHARLESTON MAGAZINE by Suzannah Smith Miles

"There was a time in the history of our country, a 13-year period between 1920 and 1933, when a pesky inconvenience called Prohibition was made law. This was a nationwide ban on the manufacture, sale, and transportation of alcoholic beverages—except for the religious wine served at communion. Across the land, citizens lawfully put away their bottles of aged Kentucky bourbon and dutifully pulled out the teacups. People forgot their fondness for their afternoon gin and tonic and settled instead for tall glasses filled with sassafras and soda.

Well, some did. From time immemorial, Charlestonians have shown a propensity for the enjoyment of alcoholic beverages. What's more, they have few compunctions when it comes to flaunting laws with which they disagree. Prohibition? A nuisance, no question about it, but did it stop drinking in this town? Not in the least. People not only continued to imbibe, but with a tradition dating to the days of the Confederate blockade runners, the Lowcountry became a hotbed for rum-running and the manufacture of a home-brewed corn whiskey called "moonshine."

While backwoods bootleggers were active across the state during Prohibition, one place outshined them all. Hell Hole Swamp in Berkeley County became so famous for the corn liquor made in its hinterlands that it gained a national reputation. "Berkeley County is a festering sore in South Carolina," ranted the state's pious and fervently dry Governor John G. Richards in 1929. A rabid prohibition-ist, Richards had gained even less popularity two years prior when he resurrected a blue law dating from 1700 making selling gasoline and playing golf illegal on Sundays. Richards was so determined to wipe clean the stills of Hell Hole Swamp that in 1930, Charleston newsman Tom Waring Jr. wrote, "Hell Hole Swamp, exuding an aroma of spiritu-ous liquors which reeked throughout the Southeast, was a stench in his nostrils."

Despite Richards' attempts to drain Hell Hole Swamp of its high-ly profitable bootlegging business—and the repeated raids by the state and federal revenue agents known as "Prohi" men—the illegal corn-li-quor trade flourished. Mason jars filled with Hell Hole Swamp moon-shine were shipped by the boxcar-full to Al Capone's Chicago, lined the shelves of speakeasies in New York, and filled the teacups at the blind tigers in Columbia, Savannah, and Atlanta. Closer to home, it kept the citizens of Charleston in the afternoon cocktails to which they were long accustomed. As one elder matriarch of Holy City society quipped, "Of course we continued to drink during Prohibition. I don't know where Daddy bought the liquor. It was just delivered to the back porch every morning with the milk."

Hell Hole Swamp

While there are probably topographical maps showing distinct geo-graphic boundaries for Hell Hole Swamp, the name generally refers to an area of forlorn and unforsaken swamplands and dense, piney woods that stretch from Jamestown on the Santee River to Moncks Corner on the Cooper River, and from Awendaw and Cainhoy upwards to Huger, Cordesville, and St. Stephen.

From the beginning of colonial settlement, this misbegotten area has been called "Hell Hole;" the name shows up on maps that predate the Revolutionary War. In fact, General Francis Marion gained fame for the ease with which he and his partisan rangers eluded the British in Hell Hole's murky recesses, earning the nickname, "Swamp Fox."

Even today, Hell Hole Swamp is better left to the alligators, bears, bobcats, foxes, snakes, panthers, and other denizens that crawl, slither, and stalk its indefinite boundaries. Hell Hole is the rightful domain of the water moccasin and anvil-headed rattlesnake. Its air is choked with swarms of mosquitoes and biting deer flies. Entering the treacherous mires of this wild part of the Lowcountry is not for the faint-hearted or inexperienced. If you don't get lost, you will assuredly get bitten by something. With luck, the worst will be a rash of chigger bites.

There was a time that this region had a wealth and prosperity brought by the great rice plantations that once lined the rivers. Starting in the late 1600s, the French Huguenots were among the earliest to settle these lands, joined by colonists from the British Isles and the Caribbean. The swamps were tamed into rice fields, reaping profits that bought the planters town houses in Charleston and sent their sons to England for education and their daughters to finishing schools and on European tours.

The Civil War changed all that. By the 1920s, the plantations were in ruins and the rice fields had reverted back to swamps. Hell Hole had been left behind, forgotten. Those with better sense had long since fled to Charleston or Columbia, any place where a reasonable livelihood could be made. Those who remained were a hardy lot, but some had become almost as feral as the swamp. "People there became a hard, unkempt, and illiterate race, ignorant and superstitious, but with a pioneer's jealous love of freedom," wrote Waring. Far removed from their cultured antecedents, they had been changed by time, isolation, and a lack of education.

Hell Hole's Prohibition-era inhabitants lived a hardscrabble existence in dogtrot cabins with tar-paper roofs and newspaper-covered interior walls. There was often an outhouse in the yard and a blue-tick hound asleep in the dirt under the sagging front porch. Behind the house, there was a garden where tomatoes, beans, and the essential stand of tall corn grew. And back yonder in the woods, hidden in the swamp, was the still.

Corn liquor had been made by the people of Hell Hole Swamp for ages. Most families had their own recipes, their own special products with distinct tastes. Prohibition made little difference to them. For that matter, sometimes the "law" was a brother-in-law or uncle who gladly turned a blind eye. Thus when people from Charleston came knocking at the door, looking for raw "still juice" to take home and age in charred kegs, they gladly made the sale.

As Prohibition dragged on, sales became more numerous. So did the number of stills. For years moonshine had been a household commodity—now it was profitable. Rusty trucks and automobiles filled with brimming mason jars rattled down the dirt roads to all parts of the state. The whole region was getting happily drenched in Hell Hole corn whiskey.

Business was booming. "Stills sprang up like mushrooms," wrote Waring. "Sandy farms which never had been productive were abandoned. It was much easier to run a still." But Governor Richards had other plans for the residents of Hell Hole who were so blatantly ignoring the law. And, as in any bull market, competition became keen. Soon the fighting between rival families grew as hot as the boilers cooking the mash.

Fox In The Henhouse

One of the enterprising magnates of the Hell Hole moonshine business was kingpin Glennie McKnight. He furnished the equipment, sugar, and cornmeal to the men who ran the stills and took care of distribution and marketing. At all steps of the process, "McKnight corn" was putting money into everybody's pockets. Others within the McKnight organization were his brother, Sammie, and their friends, the Mitchums and Johnsons. Among McKnight's rivals were the Ben Villeponteaux clan, which included his cronies, the Wrights and Andersons. The feud between the two groups turned violent.

On May 8, 1926, they came to blows on a highway near Moncks Corner in a regular gangland-style shoot-out. Glennie McKnight came out unhurt, but his brother, Sammie, was killed, as was Jervey Mitchum. Ben Villeponteaux was seriously wounded, as were Jeremiah Wright and James Anderson. Less than two weeks later, another ambush shooting near the little crossroads town of Huger killed LeGrand Cumbee and seriously wounded his father, the "king of Hell Hole Swamp," Sabb Cumbee.

The gunfights in "bloody Berkeley" made national news, and the Federal government decided to take action. While there had been efforts by the state government to enforce Prohibition in Hell Hole Swamp, they had been half-hearted and largely ineffective. Agents would occasionally blunder onto a still and destroy it. Mostly, though, they got lost in the swamp's wild morasses. The Feds realized they needed someone who knew the territory, a man familiar with the bootlegging families and the wilds of Hell Hole Swamp to lead the effort. They hired none other than the kingpin himself, Glennie McKnight.

Why McKnight became involved is probably still up for discussion. Some say he took the job to avoid a Federal indictment. Others claim he sought revenge for his brother's murder. Almost all agree it provided him with a legal way to destroy rival stills. Whatever the reason, McKnight put on his badge and went to work.

On September 3, 1926, the Coast Guard cutter Yamacraw carrying 100 Federal agents entered Charleston Harbor. The following day, led by McKnight, they invaded Hell Hole Swamp. The raid took two days and resulted in the arrest of 33 men (including a sheriff and a deputy) and the destruction of 17 stills. Thousands of gallons of whiskey were poured onto the ground.

More raids followed during the year that McKnight worked for the Feds. On the local and state level, the raids were considered a success; however, the U.S. Senate was not impressed. Moonshine was still gushing out of Hell Hole Swamp. As newsman Waring wrote, "The stream of white corn whiskey still flowed from that valley of a thousand smokes, where nearly every smoke marked a still."

Infighting & Politics

"Do you mean to say you hired the king of the bootleggers to be a Prohibition officer?" gasped Senator K. D. McKellar of Tennessee, a member of the U.S. Senate's Brookhart Committee, which was investigating the numerous discrepancies uncovered with the Hell Hole Swamp raids. The more the Senate probed into the Prohibition-ignoring moonshiners of Hell Hole, the more they became displeased.

"Bootlegging continues," attested state constable J. L. Poppenheim. "McKnight may have cleaned up part of the county, but it didn't help much." Indeed, after McKnight turned in his badge, he went right back into the bootlegging business.

The findings of the Brookhart Committee's investigations and later hearings in Columbia brought even greater gasps of astonishment and not a few sniggers of amusement. It was becoming evident that law-enforcement officers, from sheriffs to deputies, had either been buying corn whiskey, selling it, or giving seized whiskey away to their friends. Even squeaky-clean Governor Richards became involved: His own son-in-law had been found transporting whiskey across the state after leaving a deer hunt near Hell Hole Swamp; four bottles of Hell Hole liquor had been put in his car trunk by Berkeley County deputy sheriff W. E. Woodward.

Enraged, Governor Richards ordered Sheriff C. P. Ballentine to fire Woodward. When Ballentine refused, Richards ordered Ballentine removed from office. Ballentine, who was an elected official, appealed to the Supreme Court, saying the governor did not hold such executive privilege. Meanwhile, the governor also accused Ballentine and Woodward of not only selling seized liquor but imbibing it themselves. In the end, the Supreme Court decided with the governor. Ballentine was out.

Clouds were also beginning to gather around Berkeley County's state senator, Edward J. Dennis. The Feds, still on the hunt, called in Ballentine and Woodward to testify about what was really going on in Berkeley County. The real people in the whiskey business, they said, were none other than Senator Dennis and the state constables (purportedly members of the Anderson-Villeponteaux gang) who Dennis had personally asked the governor to appoint as Prohibition agents.

Ballentine's and Woodward's testimonies were damning. They explained how Dennis and his cronies were getting rich through a foolproof system that operated on many levels. It worked like this: The constables would arrest a moonshiner and seize his whiskey. They then sold the whiskey to their own bootleggers. Senator Dennis, who was a lawyer, made his money through attorney's fees when he represented the moonshiners who'd been caught. Given his influence, Dennis could arrange to have the cases dropped, but only for a "consideration." These fees, said Ballentine and Woodward, amounted to nothing short of paying tribute to the "king of the bootleggers."

A special investigator and prosecuting attorney were appointed. Indictments were issued against Senator Dennis and the constables. The trial was held in Charleston, with a long line of moonshiners parading across the witness stand, most of whom substantiated the charges.

It was all nonsense, testified the senator. Who could believe bootleggers, anyway? With a brilliant defense that included testimonies from congressmen and some of the foremost lawyers of the state, the jury eventually brought in a verdict of acquittal. Throughout it all, corn whiskey poured from the stills in Hell Hole Swamp. Raids continued but with the same, ineffectual results. And the bitterness between rivals festered.

This came to another bloody climax when, on the morning of July 24, 1930, as Senator Dennis was walking to his office in Moncks Corner, 30-year-old W. L. "Sporty" Thornley placed a shotgun on the radiator of his car and fired a load of buckshot into the senator's brain. The senator died the following day.

Thornley was arrested, as was his brother, Curtis, and Fred Artis, the bodyguard of Glennie McKnight. Sporty, who was described in newspaper articles as a "tubercular, disabled, World War I veteran" and town loafer with the "intelligence of a boy of 12," later testified that it was Glennie McKnight who had furnished him with the gun. For shooting Dennis, McKnight had promised Sporty cash, protection, and a house for his family. McKnight was also arrested. Yet in the end, only Sporty was convicted and given a life sentence.

Moonshining continued and McKnight and his rivals continued to profit from the stills of Hell Hole Swamp. McKnight, himself, barely avoided death. In May 1930, he was wounded by a hail of gunshot as he was leaving his home. In late April 1932, McKnight was ambushed again, his car riddled with bullets as he pulled away from a store in Huger.

Prohibition was finally repealed in 1933. Now that liquor was legal, the flow of big money into Hell Hole Swamp ceased. As for the backwoods stills? The Hell Hole residents continued to enjoy, and sell, the white corn liquor they concocted in the swamp's murky interiors. In all likelihood, they still do.

Al Capone

Hell Hole Swamp was purportedly one of the biggest suppliers of illegal liquor to Chicago during Prohibition. Stories abound about how racketeer Al Capone would arrive in a fancy limo with his henchmen and wads of money "to take care of business." Moonshine kingpins Glennie McKnight and Jerry "Foxy" Christian would buy all the corn whiskey they could from local bootleggers and ship it to Chicago in railroad boxcars. One yarn tells of the time Capone didn't pay for a shipment sent up by McKnight. When McKnight refused to send more, Capone supposedly sent six Cadillacs filled with his toughest hoods down to teach the Hell Hole moonshiners a lesson. McKnight's boys led the gangsters in their leather shoes and fancy suits into the swamp and left them there after taking their money and their cars.

Moonshining: A Glossary

MOONSHINE: The word is an adaptation of the word "moonrakers," an archaic term for early English smugglers; of course, it was also inspired by the fact that in order to avoid discovery, most distillation was done at night by the light of the moon.

BOOTLEGGER: Some state that the term hearkens back to the age of sail and the smugglers' custom of hiding packages of valuables in their large sea-boots to avoid detection. Others attribute it to the Civil War, when soldiers would sneak liquor into army camps by concealing pint bottles in their boots or beneath their trouser legs.

SPEAKEASY: The name given to saloons during Prohibition (they were also known as "speak softly shops") arose from the practice of speaking quietly in public about a place that sold illegal alcoholic beverages.

BLIND TIGER: Also called a "blind pig," it was the term for establishments that sold alcohol without a license. To circumvent the law, they would charge customers to see an attraction, such as an animal, and then serve a "complimentary" alcoholic beverage.

RUM-RUNNING: The many inlets and rivers on the Lowcountry coast made running liquor in from Canada, Bermuda, and the Caribbean a profitable business. Charleston newspapers often reported the discovery of "red liquor," wine, and various imported whiskeys that "exchanged hands" in Berkeley County and Charleston.

Others simply smuggled in labels. Under the headline of "Foreign Labels on Moonshine," one newspaper report told of agents who raided an abandoned house near Moncks Corner and found "several hundred empty bottles bearing Canadian Club and other labels, a considerable quantity of wrapping paper with similar designs, a supply of corks, loose labels, sealing wax, mucilage, caps, seals, and other supplies, together with several hundred empty fruit jars whose odor indicated that ordinary moonshine had recently been poured from them.

APPENDIX H

THE BERKELEY INDEPENDENT, Moncks Corner, S.C., April 14, 1993

Special course helps deputies improve writing

By Mary Beth Martin
Independent Features Editor

While they're not writing the "great American novel," 10 Berkeley County Sheriff's Deputies recently completed a unique English course to help them improve their written reports.

The six-week course was designed especially for law enforcement officers by Berkeley County Adult Education and may be the first course of its type in the state, Sheriff Ray Isgett said.

Isgett said he asked Adult Education for help after learning some officers and supervisors had problems writing incident reports and had difficulty passing courses required for certification at the state Criminal Justice Academy.

In their reports, officers have to deal with legal materials and forms, as well as write narrative accounts of incidents for court. Officers' reports must also conform to State Law Enforcement Division requirements in order to stand up in court.

Paper work for a reportable offense can take 30 minutes or more to complete and may include an incident report and supplements, booking report, property inventory and a prosecutive summary for the solici-

administrative officer Maj. Hubert Harrell.

"Police officers can't be functionally illiterate. Officers must be able to describe in writing what they see and hear," Harrell said.

In response, Jean McCrary, the comunity education coordinator, developed a course designed to meet the specific needs of law enforcement officers. Common problems in written reports included spelling and grammar errors and repeating extraneous information.

All course materials, practice examples and homework assignments dealt with law enforcement and types of writing an officer must do. The instructor described scenarios and had the deputies write them as if they were doing an incident report, then they would discuss the examples in class.

Officers attended two-hour classes twice a week for six weeks, and also had homework assignments to complete. They attended class on their own time, in addition to their regular duties.

Harrell said he saw improvement in the deputies' reports after just two weeks in the class. He credited the course instructor Carol King with making the course a suc-

"Some of our deputies resisted going to the class. They thought there would be a stigma against them for having to take a remedial class. Carol King set them straight at the first meeting. She treated them like adults, not dummies. Her no nonsense approach earned their respect right away. In the end, they gave her an A+."

The sheriff was so impressed with the course, he said he planned to submit it to the Criminal Justice Academy as a possible model for its officer training program.

Harrell agreed, "This is an example of what can happen when county agencies pool their resources, and the school district did not charge us a bundle either. In return, we will be doing some programs in the schools."

Harrell believes the English class will have benefits beyond helping deputies write clearer reports. "The best police officers have to have good communication skills to do the job right. It takes more than just being a tough guy."

The first session of the class began March 2 and a second session of the course will be offered in late April. Adult Education may do separate classes for deputies and jail personnel because they write different types of reports.

APPENDIX I

Evening Post Article by Arlie Porter

10-A — The Evening Post, Charleston, S.C., Thursday, October 4, 1990

Berkeley Sheriff's Race Heating Up

By ARLIE PORTER
Of the Post-Courier staff

A joke about the Berkeley County Sheriff's department drew sparks rather than laughs Wednesday.

Incumbent Berkeley County Sheriff M.C. Cannon said his opponent, Ray Isgett, has compared brown and tan sheriff's patrol cars to Snickers candy bars: "chocolate and caramel on the outside and a nut on the inside."

Isgett, however, said he didn't approve of the remark either, and said he has emphasized that good deputies work for the sheriff.

The men, speaking at a candidates forum sponsored by the Moncks Corner chapter of the National Association for the Advancement of Colored People and attended by about 70 people, sparred over campaign techniques and the county's fight against drugs.

"I can't afford to pay somebody $5,000 to ... degrade my opponent," Cannon said, suggesting that is what Isgett did. "And I will not do that."

In response to questions about combating drug use, Cannon said he is the first Berkeley County sheriff to form a narcotics unit and that, in seven months last year, drugs valued at more than $16 million were destroyed by his department.

Isgett, a criminal investigator with S.C. Electric & Gas Co., emphasized that solving the county's drug problems should begin with education, and include involvement of churches, schools and communities.

He also said he played a key role in implementing the crime watch program throughout the state, which has proven successful in the fight against drugs.

Isgett said the sheriff's department should be held accountable for spending money confiscated through drug busts, but Cannon said that may jeopardize deputies' or informants' lives.

M.C. Cannon

County supervisor candidate William "Pee Wee" Peagler, a Democrat and currently county probate judge, said that, in his 16 years as probate judge, he has become known as a "servant of the people." James Rozier, a Republican and owner of a cemetery, said that he

Ray Isgett

may not be well known now, but that he should be by the election. He said the county needs an able administrator to handle an $18.4 million budget.

Republican Robert Glover, running against incumbent Democrat James F. Dangerfield for the County Council District 4 seat, said he would have a liaison in every community "to help me do my job better." Dangerfield cited his 10 years experience on council.

Glover said that the county needs a land use plan. Dangerfield and council members Julius Barnes and Bernice Friendly, both Democrats,

said they were against such a plan. Barnes is running unopposed, while Mrs. Friendly faces Republican Steve Vaughn, who didn't attend the forum.

Coroner candidate Milton Scott said he would improve response time and conditions at the county morgue, while challenger Wade Arnette said he would modernize the office. Scott, a Democrat, is president of Holman-Scott Funeral Home in Moncks Corner. Arnette, who cited his administrative experience, is a statistician with the S.C. Department of Insurance.

Register of Mesne Conveyence candidate and Democrat Mildred Hood said she would seek to computerize the office. Mrs. Hood is now deputy clerk of court. Republican challenger Cynthia Forte said she has served 19 years as deputy RMC, and she already has the experience necessary to run the office.

Probate Judge candidate William Hitto said he would further train employees, computerize the office, and assure that the office has good relations with attorneys, physicians and police.

"We already have all that," opponent Nancy Whaley said. Mrs. Whaley said she has been associate probate judge for over 13 years, and already knows how the office runs.

Clerk of Court Mary Brown said in the eight years she has served, she has computerized the office, and provided accountability in spending. Mrs. Brown's challenger, Republican Joan Moore, did not attend the forum Mrs. Moore is a school secretary.

APPENDIX J

The Post and Courier

BUSINESS

Berkeley industry-seekers hit triple

, 1996

NUCOR THE LURE: Three new firms join the Berkeley County industrial cluster.

By CHRIS SOSNOWSKI
The Post and Courier staff

Three companies on Tuesday formally joined the burgeoning Berkeley County industrial cluster anchored by Nucor Corp.

Charleston Regional Development Alliance Chairman T. Graham Edwards made the announcement at the Trident Research Center that MG Industries Inc., Charleston Mill Service and Marine Terminals are locating operations at the Cainhoy mill.

They bring $48 million in capital invest-ment and 115 direct new jobs to the area. "They would not be here if not for Nucor," he said.

"A successful cluster is one that produces spinoffs," said Suzie Commerce Secretary Robert V. Royall "It takes a team. It takes allies to produce clusters."

Royall said clusters are helping to rejuve-nate South Carolina's economy and are very much a part of our future. Projections indi-cate the growth of the industrial complex around steelmaker Nucor will create 1,100 jobs and $100 million in economic develop-ment, he said.

"We've hit a triple and the bases are still loaded," said Berkeley County Supervisor Jim Rozier.

A subsidiary of Hoechst Celanese, MG In-dustries Inc. of Malvern, Pa., has invested about $37 million in its new 10-acre plant on a site leased from Nucor, and expects to in-vest another $6 million over the next two years, said MG Industries area manager Al Bentz. Up to 55 employees will be hired to supply gaseous oxygen, argon and nitrogen to Nucor for its steel-melting process.

Echoing Graham, Bentz said the company located here because Nucor was the best of several potential spots considered world-wide. Adding to that was the fact that Berke-ley County is a draw for other businesses, he said.

Likewise, Nucor was the honey that at-tracted Marine Terminals of South Carolina Inc. said its president, David Stone. A sister company, Marine Terminals of Arkansas, al-ready has a working relationship with Nucor, which Stone called "America's premier recy-cler."

The operation brings a $5 million invest-ment and will employ about 30 people to provide barge services for inbound area metal and outgoing finished products.

Charleston Mill Service, a subsidiary o Edward C. Levy Co. of Detroit, is a family based company with a $6 million local in-vestment in its slag steel and metal recover operation.

The company takes the molten slag by product from steel production and processe it to be reused in paving asphalt, said Bruc E. Roth, Levy Co. vice president.

Of the 30 people expected to be hired a startup begins next month, 18 come from th tri-county area. Roth said he expects 15 per-cent to 20 percent growth in the next few years.

APPENDIX K

A conversation with Jim Rozier

Editor's note: Jim Rozier has been Berkeley County's supervisor — its top administrator and head of County Council — since 1991. Neighborhood Editor Robert Behre recently reviewed him about this county's future political plan.

Post and Courier: What is the biggest issue facing Berkeley County today?

Rozier: Gosh, there are so many things that we're working on, but I guess the big thing we're working on is our green-space plan, our preservation of land. We're putting together a pretty significant program on that. Already 28 percent of the county is protected, and our goal is 50 percent. We think it's pretty exciting.

P&C: How does that differ from the biggest issue when you first took office in 1991?

Rozier: The biggest issue I faced at that point was creating jobs. I think they're creating jobs and protecting land complement each other. We've been careful at what kind of industry we've brought in.

Now we put 5,000 acres in protection. When you bring good industry in — Bayer and Dupont and all the others work very well with us on that. Oftentimes, people don't see it that way.

P&C: Berkeley County came out against a large, new proposed container terminal on Daniel Island — this after years of emphasis on industrial recruitment. Does this reflect a major shift?

Rozier: No, I think what we've actually said was that the port needs to grow and the port needs to prosper, but we offered several alternatives they should consider. More than just saying we were against it, we gave some suggestions on some alternative opportunities.

P&C: You mentioned the county's plans for protecting rural land. What else is the county going to balance economic growth with concerns about sprawl and quality of life?

Rozier: The whole county has zoning now, which allows us to more guide and direct that growth. We've got a comprehensive plan put in place that also guides and directs that growth. I don't think you stop growth, I don't think you control it. I think you manage it.

P&C: Berkeley County government has grown under your tenure, but growth has helped prevent any tax increase. Will it become harder for the county to keep taxes down? Why or why not?

Rozier: When you say Berkeley County government has grown, I think we've grown fairly slowly. I went from 34 directors to 18 directors. I reduced the number of directors and increased the amount of responsibility. When I first took office, our income from fees in lieu of taxes was $700,000. This year, it's over $12 million. As long as we continue to bring industry in, I think we can continue to hold the line on taxes. It's going to be a management effort. It's going to take a lot of good management.

P&C: You supported the Berkeley County School District's recent bond referendum. Do you feel the quality of schools is becoming more important to Berkeley's economic future?

Rozier: Absolutely. I think it's always been important, but I think it's more important now because it's in the minds of everybody today. It's in the forefront today. In Berkeley County, I don't know if you know it or not, but our test scores are rising. They're going through the roof.

P&C: Is there anything you can do as supervisor to promote that, or do you think it's largely out of your hands?

Rozier: I think the thing I can do as county supervisor is, through economic development efforts, to bring in good tax base and good jobs and good industry. I think my effort will be to continue to bring in good jobs, good industry, good opportunities and a good tax base.

P&C: When you announced for re-election in 1998, you mentioned you would like to see a water park built. Where does that stand?

Rozier: We're working on a path. We're in the process of talking about a park now up from Lake Moultrie or Lion's Beach. It would be a pretty significant park — about a 308-acre park. It would not just be a water park, but would also have walkways, cabins, other recreational entities and so forth.

When North Charleston's Wannamaker Park opened with plans for a water park, that changed our plans for a large water park because we wouldn't build one quite that big. But recreation is one of the things we're working on pretty steadily right now.

P&C: What do you enjoy most about your job?

Rozier: Working with people. I'm a people person and trying to help with the needs and concerns and problems they have.

P&C: What frustrates you the most?

Rozier: Trying to communicate with all the people — trying to get the message out about what's really happening. There's so much distrust of government today — it seems the favorite pastime is beat on government. Trying to communicate with 140,000 people, it's tough. I wish I could sit down and talk with them like I'm talking with you.

P&C: Do you have any regrets about opting out of the governor's race so early?

Rozier: No. No. If it is something that comes along as an opportunity again, I might look at it. But right now, I think the place for me is where I am, and I plan to run for supervisor again.

P&C: Do you know who you will be backing for governor?

Rozier: It's a little early for me to get involved in that. I've got a sitting governor I need to work with on behalf of Berkeley County.

P&C: You already have announced you will seek reelection in two years. Any guesses what the big issue will be at that time?

Rozier: No. Whatever the big issue is, we'll deal with it. We're working with the things we think are the right things to work with. I don't even know who might be running against me in two years but I haven't had a free ride yet.

ABOUT THE AUTHOR

B. Earl Copeland, Author

Earl graduated from Lynchburg High School in 1959. He attended a small community business school before deciding to apply for an airline job. He enrolled in Universal Airline Career School in Miami, Florida. Upon completing the course, in 1963 he applied for and was hired by Eastern Airlines in Charleston, S. C. He worked for that company for twenty-seven years, until the company declared bankruptcy in 1991.

While working for Eastern, he coached youth baseball, and became interested in politics. He wrote a youth sports column, and letters to the editor for the local weekly newspaper, Hanahan News, about local political issues. The editor invited him to write a freelance political column titled One Man's Opinion, which he did for several years.

In 1975, four days before the City of Hanahan election, the candidate he was supporting for mayor met with an untimely accidental death. A group of his supporters asked Copeland to allow his name to be entered as a write-in candidate since it was too late to have his name included on the ballot. Some members of that group had previously approached Copeland about running for mayor, but he had decided against it. He agreed, and four days later he was elected as mayor of Hanahan.

During his time as mayor, he took a leave of absence from Eastern, but returned to his career at the end of his term. Afterwards, beginning in

1986, he served five terms as Chairman of Berkeley County Republican Party. Following Eastern's demise in 1991, he worked on the staffs of two South Carolina governors, Carroll Campbell and David Beasley.

Copeland joined the staff of Congressman Henry Brown following the 2000 campaign in which he served as Grassroots Campaign Coordinator. When Senator Tim Scott was elected to Congress following Brown's retirement in 2010, the new congressman invited Copeland to join his staff. Copeland retired from serving on Senator Scott's staff in December 2013 at the age of 72. At age 82, he continues to serve his community in voluntary capacities, serving on two nonprofit boards.

Milton Keynes UK
Ingram Content Group UK Ltd.
UKHW021449161124
451130UK00017B/144/J

9 798822 960039